lost secrets of
astrology

lost secrets of astrology

ancient divination through the influence of the stars

robert w. pelton

nash publishing, los angeles

Library of Congress Catalog Card Number: 72-95253
International Standard Book Number: 0-8402-1314-X

Published simultaneously in the United States and Canada
by Nash Publishing Corporation, 9255 Sunset Boulevard,
Los Angeles, California 90069.

Printed in the United States of America.

First Printing.

contents

preface

The great, the really overwhelming difficulty with occult astrology lies in the fact that much of its value depends on our power to interpret human nature. Unless we know how the mind of man works, astrology makes no revelation to us. Supersensitive people are able to read the very soul of life, even when relatively uneducated, simply by utilizing their natural intuitive faculties. Astrology serves as a rough guide, enabling them to make predictions that stagger our very senses. And for the same reason, the most astute thinkers and men of infinite learning, fail in the art of astrology, lacking the intuition so necessary to follow the complex fluctuations of human thought, feeling, and life, in general.

The case is the same with great art and literature. The most learned man cannot paint a picture or write a novel of any value unless he has this unanalyzable, intuitive knowledge which, according to Ptolemy, is a "gift of the gods." In precisely the same way, prediction in astrology may be called an art form. It, too, requires delicate intuitiveness to reveal accurate truths.

The pages of history tell us of diviners who were accused of casting evil spells on many kings and rulers, and who practiced occult astrology until they were made to pay the supreme penalty by the disgruntled person in power at the time. The merciless Robespierre, and his Reign of Terror in the late eighteenth century; Bernadotte, the French general who subsequently advanced to the Swedish throne; Wallenstein, Duke of Friedland and Mecklenburg; and Murat, King of Naples—these are a few who felt the spell of astrological fortune-telling and retaliated.

The history of astrological divination goes back many centuries. Dozens of theories, some bordering on the ridiculous, are advanced as to the source from which these methods of divination arrived in Europe. It has been established that people of ancient China and India possessed many methods which differed widely, both in actual use and material design, from the popular methods adopted in the western world at a much later date. Occult lore and technique are so ancient, that it is practically impossible to trace their origins.

Although there are some who make fun of these things, there are very few among us who do not feel somewhat uneasy, disturbed, or a little restless when we are brought face to face with an example of the uncanny, seemingly magical powers of occult astrology. Everyone can well afford to laugh at the occult sciences while the sun is shining brightly in their lives, and when all is well. But there come those dark days of illness and depression in the lives of all people, days when many may well be forced, through circumstances, to seek out the assistance of these mysterious forms of divination.

Many people, unfortunately, have used astrological divining methods to extort money or gifts from the ignorant and the gullible. This gift of the gods, more often than not, has been totally vulgarized and debased for the advantage of the insincere and the criminal. Yet, with some practitioners, it is still carefully guarded and held aloft as a sacred faith, that is believed to be no more superstitious and incredulous than some perverted forms of Christianity.

Those who may be somewhat unstable emotionally, or morbid in personality and general outlook, should beware of letting occult astrology play too important a part in their personal lives. We should feel no pangs of shame over sensing a certain fear of the unknown and the supernatural—but, neither should we be so gullible as to accept any one method of divination as the rule and guiding light of life.

Logic tells us that astrological divination, by whatever method, is nothing more than the belief in things of the supernatural realm, and that it is, assuredly, unrealistic to expect inspiring revelations. Yet, in dealing with these astrologically based fortune-telling methods, we actually may find that something about our perplexities is more clearly discerned, and that the resultant predictions may well, unconsciously, set our feet on the right path.

There are a great number of reliable methods of astrological divination which seem to have been proven successful for centuries. Anyone observing the basic rules can learn to use them properly. A more serious study of how they are interpreted and treated while in the hands of others will always provide, if nothing else, a source of amusement. It may also provide a spiritual lift to those in need of hope instead of despair; it may lighten sorrow in the heart, and send the inquirer away with a newly felt comfort.

Interest in the mysterious occult world is having a tremendous revival internationally. This revival was initiated by the younger generation and, eventually, caught on among the older groups. A great number of well-educated, prominent individuals in all walks of life are beginning to seek help from spiritualists, occultists, and particularly from astrologers. They are having "their fortunes told" as eagerly as did the personages, great and small, of the past.

This book has been expressly compiled for use by those individuals—so numerous in the present epoch of psychic inquiry—who desire to test their intuitional faculties by utilizing astrological divinatory methods from the past.

The pages that follow are filled with information that will, hopefully, provide believers, as well as those openminded enough to read and fairly judge its contents, with a source of inspiration and interest. For nonbelievers, or those on the fringe, it cannot help but provide a great source of entertainment.

Each method of astrological fortune-telling is given for what it may be worth. The ancient seers insisted that their many unique forms of divination could be relied upon to produce truthful expositions. They expected these various methods to be taken seriously, as they, certainly, were most sincere in their personal faith. The author has no desire to detract from these views.

Whatever you, the reader, decide to do with occult astrology is your private affair: It may be an amusing pastime flavored with a strong seasoning of mystery; it may be utilized as a test of your intuitive skill, an experience in the mysterious laws of chance and coincidence.

The major aim of the author has been simply to collect what is readily understood, practical, supported by magical authority, and in accordance with mystical doctrine. Some of these materials are presented for the first time in the English language. These, in particular, have been gleaned from many remote and comparatively unknown sources. Each method of divination is offered at face value. Each should be tested through experience. No specific claim is made concerning any of them.

to doubt the influence of the stars
is to doubt the wisdom and providence of god.
tycho brahe (1546-1601)

lost secrets of
astrology

BOOK I
astropalmistry

The term chiromancy (from *chir,* hand, and *mancie,* to pre-dict) is that portion of astrological science that foretells events and circumstances by certain lines or marks in the hand.

The hands are divided, astrologically, into three principal parts: the palm, the hollow, and the fingers. These three major divisions are further subdivided by specific lines, marks and prominences which are under the influence of the planets, Saturn, Sol, Jupiter, Mars, Venus, Mercury, Luna, and the twelve signs of the zodiac, as shown in the accompanying illustration.

Certain prominences, which are called "mounts" or tuber-cula, are found at the root of each finger. These, too, are named after the planets. The first mount in the Map of the Palm is called the *Mount of Mercury.* This is seen to be at the root of the little finger and it is supposed to be under the direct influence of that particular planet.

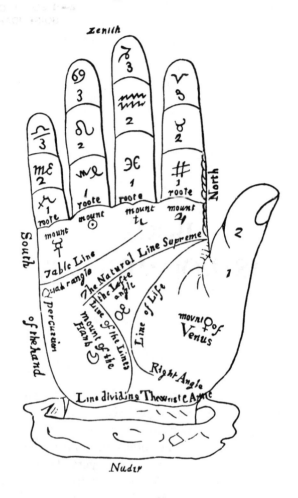

Figure 1

   This unique Map of the Palm was first published in the United States in 1854, in a privately printed book entitled, Mysteries of Astrology, *by Dr. C. W. Roback. It is believed to have originated, sometime during the early part of the sixteenth century, in an old English manuscript.*

Mercury governs the rational and intellectual faculties to a large degree. He is the source of wit, ingenuity, invention, skill in the arts and sciences, discovery, and all the important branches of human knowledge. If this mount is large, the person is highly intelligent, alert, and quick to make decisions and take appropriate action. This mount should be relatively well developed in businessmen, especially very successful ones.

When the Mount of Mercury is excessively developed, the mind is shrewd, and its cleverness is utilized to cheat, defraud, and, possibly, even to rob and steal. A cunning, deceitful nature is exposed. If a spot occurs on this mount, trouble can be expected. If it is very small, or practically nonexistent, it signifies that drive and ambition are lacking and that success will not be forthcoming. If it is of regular height and proportions, perseverance and consistency is indicated. Such a person will not be sentimental, and will be quite serious-minded; he will be a faithful friend and a disbeliever in superstition.

Cross-lines on this mount denote a fickle love life and much indecisiveness throughout life. An island appearing on this mount shows poor business capacity and little success in financial matters. An x-like mark denotes a deceptive aptitude and possible criminal leanings. A grille signifies wrong doing, a serious mistake, or an impending accident. A star here would show a pilfering nature. A square, if reddish tinted, denotes an escape from fire. If accompanied by a star, an escape from being murdered. A triangle signifies political power or scientific and business success. If certain lines originate at the base of the little finger, and appear to be crooked on the Mount of Mercury, the person will possess a desire to rob and cheat friends and enemies alike.

If the hand is carefully examined, the initial letters of the twelve signs of the zodiac may be found within the boundaries designated for them on the illustration. These are called Sacred Letters, and are signs of good or evil influences wherever they exist. For example, the letter A (the first letter of Aries, the Ram) impressed on the Mount of Mercury, signifies that a great deal of wealth will be obtained through education and learning. If the letter C (the first letter of Cancer, the Crab) is found on the same mount, it signifies a deep knowledge of chemistry or other scientific subjects.

The next mount described is that of the *Sun, Sol,* or *Apollo,* which will be found at the base of the next or ring finger. This mount refers to artistic tastes and talents. If large, it denotes aesthetic tastes and a love for beautiful things, as well as one who enjoys much pleasure in life. If extremely large, a tendency to overindulge in luxury and extravagance is evident. Such persons have a tendency to be rather boastful. When this mount is small, it indicates a lack of energy and ambition. Such individuals have no specific goal and they tend to be gross and sensual.

The sign of a cross on this mount denotes the disposition of a miser and one who places wealth above all else in life. A fork occuring here would indicate satisfaction with things as they are. A grille signifies that the person will be a great talker, but somewhat deceitful. An island indicates grave misfortune, gossip, a scandal, and a possible danger to life itself. A star signifies wealth, but not necessarily happiness. A square promotes success in matters pertaining to art. A triangle denotes artistic tendencies and eventual success in this line of endeavor.

If there are lines passing from the Mount of Apollo to the Table Line (at present known as the Line of the Heart), and if these lines are not intersected by any cross lines, they signify great talkativeness and wit. Such fluency will eventually lead to the acquisition of wealth, and connections with those in high positions. If such lines are wavy or crooked, or intersected by others which cross them, poverty will be the lot of their possessor.

When lines proceed from the outer portion of the hand, and extend to the Mount of Apollo, they denote a liar, and a person who pretends to have a great deal more knowledge than he really has. If these lines are tortuous in their direction, it denotes deceitfulness, a desire to commit some felonious crime, and one who is adept at all types of dishonesty.

When a single line proceeds from the Table Line towards the first joint of the ring finger, it portends riches. If the line continues up that finger, it signifies the month in which this wealth will come. For example, the ring finger (the Finger of Apollo) represents the summer season in astropalmistry. The first or lower joint represents Virgo, the virgin, and the month of August. If the line stops at this point, the inheritance will be obtained in that month. If it proceeds to the second joint and then stops, it will take place in July, for this joint represents Leo, the lion. If this line proceeds to the third or last joint, representing Cancer, the crab, and the month of June, the financial gain will take place then.

The third mount of the hand is at the base of the middle finger which is dedicated to *Saturn,* the most powerful and malignant among the planets. When this mount is full, plump, and without any indentations, it denotes a simple disposition, or one who is not crafty. Such persons are extremely industrious and will work to the full limit of their capabilities. If excessively large, it signifies a melancholy tendency, a morbid disposition, and an unreasonable horror of death. Sadness will characterize the actions of such people, and there will be a strong desire to be left alone. Most thoughts will be of a rather serious nature, and pessimism will rule. If this mount is small, it denotes frugality, a buoyant nature, optimism, and business successes.

A cross on the Mount of Saturn signifies misfortune and accidents. A grille means trouble and sorrow. An island appearing on this mount denotes bad luck and danger. A star indicates more of the same. A square indicates that an illness will occur, and that the person will have problems with the object of his or her affections. A triangle represents pessimism and gloom.

If a line starts at the lower joint of the middle finger and proceeds across the Mount of Saturn, and is intersected at this point by two or more smaller lines, thus forming a double cross, it signifies a prison term, captivity, or some sort of slavery in chains. If only one line intersects it, the reverse is denoted.

If a line rises from the Table Line and crosses the Mount of Saturn, its possessors will spend their lives in the pursuit of wealth, but it will elude their grasp. They are destined always to be in need of more than they have.

If a married woman has five, six, or eight lines running from the mount to the first joint of the finger, it foretells the number of male children she will have before a daughter is born, and it also reveals that each male child will be poor.

Those who have numerous lines scattered around this mount are subject to all types of misfortune. This signifies infamy for both women and men in their domestic and social life.

The mount at the base of the index finger is dedicated to the planet *Jupiter,* and is directly under its influence. More powerful than any other planets except Saturn, Jupiter is the reverse of that evil power. It brings riches, honors, and success in the various pursuits of life, and its nature is freedom, generosity, and all of the nobler attributes.

If the Mount of Jupiter is large and full, it signifies great ambition and a proud spirit. Such individuals usually have strong religious leanings, and will tend to dominate. Self-confidence is a major characteristic. If the mount is small, it shows a lack of religious interest, selfishness, idleness, and bad manners. These individuals often marry beneath their stature and never for wealth.

A cross on this mount denotes impulsive and fatal love. A grille signifies a strong, overbearing disposition, and selfishness. An island appearing on this mount shows a reduction in the pride and ambition in the person. Two crosses represent honors, and a good marriage. A star signifies wealth, honors, fame, and one very successful love affair. More than one star denotes degradation. A woman possessing a star on this mount at the age of thirty-five will become wealthy and marry well. A square on this mount denotes that its possessor will be protected against errors in judgment. A triangle shows great diplomacy, and the ability to manage others.

If a line begins at the Table Line and proceeds directly to cross the Mount of Jupiter, it portends a violent and sudden death. If a female has two or more small lines running between this mount and the Mount of Saturn, and if these lines appear to be reddish in color, they denote ingenuity, and a jovial character. Such a person will run some risk of dying during childbirth.

Any mark resembling the astrological symbol of Jupiter appearing on this mount, presages great wealth by inheritance, combined with contentment and joy.

The *Mount of Venus,* as seen in the first illustration, is located on the lower, fleshy portion of the thumb. This mount is under the special guidance of the Queen of Love. It is the index of all passions and its influences are benevolent. It signifies a love for poetry, music and art, and refinement.

When the Mount of Venus appears to be full and quite large, it signifies a strong attraction for those of the opposite sex, kindness, and a person of action. Such people will appreciate all forms of beauty, and they will be excellent dancers. This indicates the extremely passionate lover, a cheerful outlook, and a pleasing personality. If the mount is small or deflated in appearance, the person will be rather dull, torpid, and unappreciative of beauty. If this mount is excessively large, it shows a gross-natured individual, and one who is inclined to be dishonorable and unreliable.

A cross on the upper part of this mount denotes true love in marriage. On the lower part of the mount it would show a tendency to wrangle with a mate. A grille appearing anywhere on this mount indicates deep affection which is not outwardly displayed. If an island appears, it signifies misfortune and anxiety brought on by someone who is dearly loved. A star located on this mount shows that the person will easily be influenced to do wrong when under the direction of the opposite sex. If a star appears in the center of this mount, it denotes happiness and deep affection. A square signifies that the person will be protected from the consequences of his or her passionate folly. A triangle on this mount shows an even temper, a loving nature, self-control, and tender affections.

If any lines pass upwards from the lower part of this mount, in the direction of the index finger, they denote good fortune, a rather carefree disposition, contentment, strong passions, affability, gracefulness, a towering imagination, and all of the lovelier qualities of nature.

Any male or female who has the sacred letter *G* impressed on this mount will be extremely intuitive, faithful yet vain, and fond of luxury in all forms. They will be refined and rather gallant. When a *T* appears on the Mount of Venus, it signifies a great love for the opposite sex, feelings sometimes too violent to be restrained. Such persons often are licentious, unrestrained, and uncontrollable when it comes to sexual matters.

The *Mount of the Moon* is found directly opposite the Mount of Venus, as can be seen in the illustration. This mount shows imaginative powers, and poetic, romantic, and idealistic tendencies in each individual. If this mount is very small, while the Mount of Venus is very large, the person will be fickle in his affections. He will love one moment and forget it the next. Indifference to romance is common. When this mount is of average size, there will be a love of travel and a fondness for the seashore. Superstition is a problem for those with small and medium mounts. They also tend to be rather melancholy and sad. If the Mount of the Moon is well elevated or large, the person will be prone to diseases affecting the nervous system and the brain, especially those that could cause paralysis of some type.

When a cross appears on this mount, it denotes three very serious conditions which are to take place at different periods in the person's life. Distress and poverty will be the first. Then wealth will come, but it will soon be lost. Thirdly, much suffering is to be endured. Such a cross also signifies one who cannot be trusted to tell the truth. A grille shows a tendency towards sadness and discontent. An island indicates that the imagination is weak and undeveloped. When stars appear on this mount, they signify danger in traveling, a treacherous character, and a person who should never be trusted. A square indicates that the person will be protected from all dangers while traveling. Triangles denote great power to assist others and general success.

If lines appear on the Mount of the Moon, and they are of a pale color, the person will be extremely unfortunate in everything he or she tries to accomplish. If these same lines are sharp and quite dark, the reverse is true.

When the sacred letter C appears to be impressed on this mount, the person will be fortunate in life. An L signifies much sickness and distress. A P denotes success in business dealings. An S indicates instability and uncertainty. A T denotes many long trips. A V signifies nobility, generosity, and great favor with the opposite sex.

We shall conclude this section on astrological palmistry with some general remarks on the bolder astrological lines in the hands, and their significations. Such lines are of extreme importance because they enter largely into the calculations of nativities. They point out the months and days of birth, the duration of a person's existence, and the moral and intellectual qualities of humanity.

If the *Natural Line Supreme* (at present known as the *Line of the Head*) terminates near the Mount of the Moon, and if this line is intersected by another, forming a cross, it denotes that the birth of the individual took place sometime during the month of June. If this line terminates on the Plain of Mars, the nativity was in March or October on a Tuesday. If this line terminates towards the Mount of Mercury, birth took place on a Wednesday in either May or August. If it terminates close to the Mount of Jupiter, a Thursday in February or November was the time of nativity. If it terminates near the Mount of Venus, nativity was on a Friday in either April or September. If it terminates near the Mount of Saturn, the birth date falls on a Saturday in either December or January. If it terminates near the Mount of Apollo, the nativity was on a Sunday in July. The reader should understand that in calculating the nativity by utilizing the above named line, it is necessary, in all cases, that other lines intersect at some point and form a cross.

If the *Line of Life* appears to be very long and quite deep, a long life with little illness is portended. If this line is colorless and rather short in length, a corresponding life with sickness and infirmities is foreseen. When the Line of Life has branches running towards the Line of the Lines (at present known as the Line of the Liver or the Line of Health), it reveals the accumulation of wealth, honors and excellent health throughout life. If the Line of Life diverges into a series of smaller, spidery-like lines, a great deal of sickness and eventual poverty in old age is predicted.

If the astrological symbol for the Sun is impressed upon the Line of Life, it signifies blindness in one or both eyes. If this line is intersected by other lines which form crosses, its possessor can expect dangers, misfortunes, pestilence, and even death. If the Line of Life forks off at a point near its center, and the forked line ascends in the general direction of the Mount of Apollo, honors through a good marriage can be expected, and much favoritism from members of the opposite sex will be seen. But if this forked line bends towards the Mount of Venus instead, wantonness, fornication, adultery, and every species of bestiality is indicated.

The *Table Line (Line of the Heart),* equally with the Line of Life, is necessary to the perfection of nativities. Long and clearly formed, this line represents nobility, generosity, liberality and a long and fruitful life. Impressed with a star, exile, imprisonment, shame, and cowardice is denoted. With a division which branches on the Mount of Jupiter, ecclesiastical preferments, great honors and dignities are portended. If this line appears with hairlike branches shooting off its end, it reveals anxiety, misfortune, vanity, deceitfulness, lying, and many miseries.

The *Line of the Lines (Line of Health)* is not always perceptible. When it is clearly seen on the palm, it starts at the root of the Line of Life, passes over to the Natural Line Supreme (Line of the Head). These three lines form an angle which contains what is accepted by astrologists as the *Plain of Mars.*

If the Line of the Lines is very straight, its possessor will enjoy wealth and prosperity. If crooked, it signifies a short life checkered with sickness and disease. If it branches in two different directions at the termination point, it reveals a possibility of liver ailments, frequent fainting spells, and violent palpitations of the heart. If it angles towards the Line of Life, such things as covetousness, deficiency of intellect and niggardliness of disposition can be expected. When a cross line appears at one of its extremities, robberies and death are not far distant.

If all three lines encompassing the *Plain of Mars* are clearly joined, such a union signifies riches, happiness, great ingenuity, and a quiet and peaceful old age. But if these three lines, or any one of them, is rather dull or ill-defined, general weakness, illnesses, and slow recoveries are noted. When any of these lines appears to be too short, and will not complete the triangle encompassing the Plain of Mars, it indicates that its possessor is doomed to folly, beggary, lying, and a premature death.

A few remarks concerning the Plain of Mars will conclude this section of the book. When this area of the palm appears to be full and fleshy, it shows an active, daring, and vigorous disposition, a person who is fond of taking charge of everything. It also denotes a hasty temper, rash actions, and a combative nature. If the palm is hollow, that is, having a small and undeveloped Plain of Mars, the person will be relatively peaceful, quiet, and contented. Such individuals are not warlike for they detest fighting.

When lines within this plain extend towards the external part of the hand, it signifies that the person lives in a constant state of alarm. If crosses appear on the plain, the person will be disposed, if not irresistibly compelled, to fight for something he or she believes in. This sign distinctly shows a tendency to destroy human life. A grille portends death by accident. An island denotes a violent and destructive nature bent on taking life. A star found on this plain signifies a warlike nature and promotion to high rank in the military service. When the plain is studded with stars, there will be poverty, misfortunes of war, danger of assassination, and many secret enemies. If a square appears on the plain, its possessor can expect eventually to be deprived of his or her liberty. A triangle merely shows that the person will be extremely successful in war and will have the necessary leadership qualities to go far in the military profession.

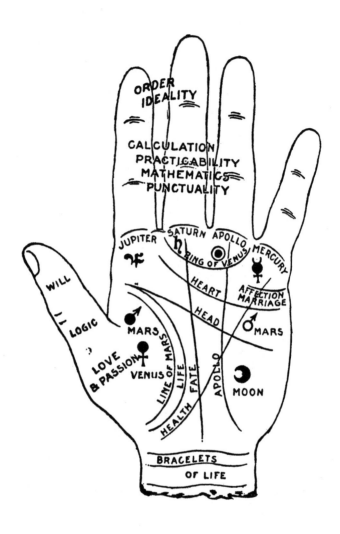

Figure 2

Another excellent illustration of a Map of the Palm, Thumb, and Fingers which dates back to the early part of the eighteenth century. This first appeared in the United States in a privately published work entitled Secrets in the Hand, *in 1902.*

BOOK II
ancient secrets of metoposcopy

Metoposcopy is simply a means of astrological divination which is accomplished by interpreting the various lines on the forehead. In this branch of predictive philosophy, as in all others, the stars exercise a potential influence. The planets are placed on the forehead, in the manner shown in Figure 3.

It must be remembered that all of these lines do not always appear on every forehead. We can draw our more particular judgments from the lines of the Sun and the Moon, as they generally do appear on most foreheads. Nevertheless, it is always much easier to analyze those individuals who possess all of the lines, than it is to judge those having only some of them.

We must carefully observe the characters that are found to represent the special mark of a planet. Such signs are infallible indications of a person's temperament, and can reveal much about a man's character as well as his future life and fortune.

These marks are crosses, semicircles, warts, stars, circles, and other such characters which are commonly found on a forehead. It should always be noted upon which planetary line these signs appear, for, without any doubt, the person shall derive something from that particular planet. In other words, the individual partakes of the nature of the planet which is most prominent in regard to his character.

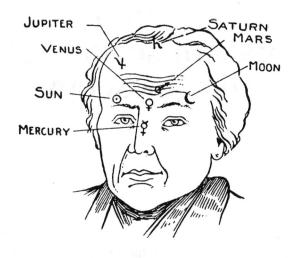

Figure 3

The above illustration, as well as all others in this section of the book, were taken from Metoposcopy, *published in London, 1609. In the above, we have the planets placed in accordance with celestial rule. Saturn is the highest, on the uppermost line near the hair. Jupiter is placed on the next line below Saturn. Then Mars falls on the third line, and Venus on the fourth, or at the root of the nose. Mercury rules the nose itself and falls directly under Venus. The Sun and the Moon rule the eyes, the Sun placed over the right eyebrow, and the Moon over the left eyebrow.*

The general significations of the planetary lines afford us the following canons and aphorisms:

1. Some of the planetary lines are fortunate symbols, while yet others are unfortunate. Those that are thought to be fortunate are the ones that are straight, or slightly bending toward the nose. They should be balanced on the forehead, continually sharp, and unbroken.

2. The unfortunate lines, or those signifying evil omens, are those that are not well defined, or those that waver and wind, and seem to resemble a semicircle, or an arc. Lines of varying depth and lines with many breaks in them are also considered to be unfortunate.

3. Simple and straight lines represent a simple, good and honest soul, a person devoid of malice.

4. The slanting or inclined line as well as lines that tend to appear distorted and that often vary in intensity, denote a great love of variety and change, a crafty nature, mischievousness, deceit, and an inclination toward thievery.

5. If the Sun line or the Moon line appears to incline sharply over the eye, feelings of enmity and maliciousness are evident.

6. A very deep and sharp Jupiter line shows good fortune in that its possessor will experience great financial gain, and will be granted recognition and honors for important contributions.

7. If the lines are sharp and straight, especially those of Saturn, Jupiter and Mars, mischievous actions, excessive love of finery and luxury, and lustfulness are strongly evident.

8. If the line of Mars exceeds all of the other lines in length and sharpness, the individual will be a natural fighter, and will make an excellent military man.

9. If a cross appears on the above-Mars line, good fortune and great successes will be found on the battlefield.

10. If a semicircle appears on the above-Mars line, misfortune is predicted, and possible death during battle.

11. If the line of Saturn is shorter than the line of Jupiter, a deeply religious nature is evident, and wealth is in store.

12. If a Saturn or Mars line appears to be broken, great misfortune is foreseen, as well as possible violent death.

13. If the line of Mercury turns down on the left side of the forehead, great misfortune is predicted, but should this same line turn downward on the right side of the forehead, it is a good omen.

14. A multitude of lines simply signify a very changeable and inconsistent individual.

15. If three or more straight lines appear where the Mercury line would normally be, expect the individual to be completely honest, reliable, and a person of integrity.

16. If the Sun or the Moon line appears to be straight, and one or both are clearly defined over the eye, travel is denoted, and the person will spend much time in places away from home.

17. Two or more Venus lines at the root of the nose which do not join together at any point, signify a lewd-minded, lust-filled person, one who is overwhelmed with passion and other vices.

18. If three or more straight lines appear where the Mercury line would normally be, and if these lines appear to bend at their extremities, gossip, deceitfulness, and unreliability are evident. Such individuals, especially the female, will be naggers, rather abusive in language, and inclined to foolishness.

19. A line that increases or decreases extensively, denotes a drastic change in the personal affairs of the person. This change will be determined by the planet represented by that particular line or lines.

20. When the line of the Sun or the Moon is perfectly formed over the eye, increased wealth and prestige is predicted.

Figure 4

According to the manuscript Metoposcopy, *1609, a prophet may be easily recognized by the appearance of four lines above the root of his nose. These lines must be deeply cut into the forehead, and must make that area appear to be wrinkled. It represents a great force "in the possession of the Spirit."*

Figure 5

The line of Jupiter, when crooked as above, denotes great wealth obtained by fraudulent and violent means. Such individuals are to never be entrusted with secrets and must be guarded against in financial dealings.

Figure 6

These lines denote the people who will be happy and very fortunate throughout their lifetimes. They will never experience poverty, although they may come close to it. Good health will predominate, and many long friendships will be made.

Figure 7

When the lines of the Sun and the Moon are joined at a point between the eyes as noted above, it signifies that the individual will experience much good fortune and very little grief in life. They are blessed with luck.

Figure 8

Such lines have a strong indication of great misfortune, for they denote many accidental injuries, especially from a multitude of falls. These people must practice much more caution before initiating things.

Figure 9

A circle as above, on the line of Jupiter, denotes a loss of wealth and an abundance of ill-fortune in every area of its possessor's life. Such individuals should expect disaster to come for they are continually courting it.

Figure 10

The position of these lines indicates a very courageous person. They possess a bold spirit and may go far in the world, yet they tend to be rather unreliable and inconsistent. Their attainment of wealth and status will be uncertain.

Figure 11

Such lines formed on a forehead signify that wealth will be made, but not accumulated. The bearer will marry many times, but will not be able to find true happiness in any union, for a selfish streak rules his life.

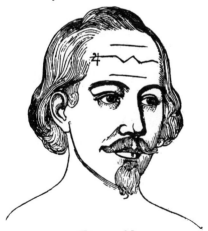

Figure 12

When a Jupiter line is clearly formed as this one is, great riches are destined for the individual. This unusual formation also signifies one who is extremely good-natured, and very prudent.

BOOK III
moles on the planetary lines of the face

All moles, wherever they may be found, are said to be the result of planetary influences or of the zodiac sign rising at birth. Moles resulting from the influence of Saturn are always black. Those given by Jupiter are of a purplish-brown color. Moles developed by the Sun are yellow; by the Moon, of a bluish-white cast; by Mercury, honey-colored; and by Venus, a very light brown; and those given by Mars, have reddish tints.

A mole that appears in the middle of the forehead and directly on the line of Saturn (see illustration, Book II), indicates that another should be located in the middle of the stomach. If such a mole is found on a woman, in any color tone, it signifies that she is of a very passionate nature, sexual-minded, and luxury loving. She is destined to suffer greatly as a result of her own folly in regard to the opposite sex.

If this same mole appears on a man, and is black in color, he will suffer much misfortune because of his deep feelings for some woman, feelings that will not be fairly returned. If the mole is red in color, he will have many problems with the opposite sex, but will derive much pleasure, just the same. If it is yellow, his most joyous experiences will result from his relationships with female companions, and there will be no outstanding problems as a result of his actions. But a pale bluish mole which appears to be raised is the best sign of all, for this signifies that the man will be extremely popular with, and much beloved by, many different women, many of whom will assist him in time of need, and console him in time of distress.

A mole found on the left side of the forehead, just beneath or on the line of Saturn, denotes that another can be found on the left side of the back. If such a mole happens to be found on a woman's face and body, in any color except black, it signifies that she will travel and live most of her life outside the country of her birth. If it also is seen to be black in tone, she is destined to be a widow.

This same mole, appearing instead on a man, denotes a life full of various disasters, and a great deal of time spent in prison. If the mole is black, he will experience general misfortune all his life; if red, trouble and eventual imprisonment will be the result of quarreling with many enemies and, even, with supposed friends; if honey colored, all his troubles will be caused from his relationships with a variety of women.

A mole found on the right side of the forehead, just beneath or on the line of Saturn, signifies that another will be seen on the right side of the breast. If this mole is found to be on a woman, except when it is black, she is destined to come into a fortune by either an inheritance or a legacy. If it happens to be black, she will have a short life-span, and will not live long enough really to enjoy her wealth.

Appearing on a man, this mole, if red, indicates that he will experience much good luck all through his lifetime, and that most of this will be the result of his great courage and forceful character; if the mole is black, his life will be generally good, but it will be continually marred by unfortunate incidents. If it is yellow, he will be able to do well in farming, or in building-construction trades. If the mole happens to be purple in color, he will unexpectedly be saddled with family responsibilities, and will be expected to make innumerable decisions regarding his own and other people's success.

A mole which is centered on the line of Jupiter, signifies that another will be found centered between the breasts. To a woman, this denotes that she is foolish, childish, and rather immature. She is prone to gossip, and will be a source of trouble to friends.

A man with such a mole is of a very harsh nature. If red in color, he will have a furious temper, and will be difficult to get along with under any circumstances. If black, he is destined to be unfortunate in every undertaking. But, should this mole be bluish in coloring, he will be a little less unlucky.

A mole appearing on the left side of the forehead, just under, or directly on the line of Jupiter, shows a woman to be imprudent in all important matters, and particularly carefree when it comes to things regarding her virtue and honor. Another mole will also appear on the left side of the stomach.

Appearing on a man, this same mole signifies an unquenchable thirst for sensual enjoyment, especially if the mole is of a purple tone. If it is honey-colored, the feelings are not quite so intense, but they are still evident to a large degree.

When a mole appears on the right side of the forehead, on or near the line of Jupiter, it indicates another located on the right side of the body, just over the liver. To a woman, this mole denotes good fortune in all that concerns her, whatever the color may be.

Such a mole on a man, in any color, indicates a very long life, many material possessions, and a fortunate and happy marriage. But, should it turn out to be black, his marriage will be a sad affair, full of disputes, and probably ending in divorce.

A mole that appears in the center of the line of Mars indicates another mole is located on the left side of the belly. This mole denotes a great deal of vanity in a woman. If it happens to be black, she will likely be the major cause of the death of some friend, but this death will be by mischance rather than by design.

Appearing on a man in any color but red, it simply indicates a deeply sensual nature, one with strong sexual appetites. If red, he is most likely to be guilty of manslaughter or even murder if he does not practice a little caution in his daily actions.

A mole appearing on the left side of the line of Mars, indicates another mole to be found on the left arm. Such a mole on a woman, whatever the color may be, signifies a serious betrayal by friends, and much misfortune in her various love affairs.

A man possessing such a mole will be argumentive in all areas of his life. But should this mole be either yellow or purple, these arguments will be concentrated on things concerning women. If black, he will also be very treacherous, and will suffer many serious losses through an insatiable thirst for gambling.

A mole seen on the right side of the line of Mars, shows that another will be found on the right arm. A woman possessing such a mole will marry well, in all probability a wealthy husband who is full of kindness and understanding. She will do well in life, and should bear a number of healthy, well-mannered children.

This same mole appearing on a man, if black, signifies extreme danger from a four-footed beast. If honey-colored, he will experience good fortune raising, or dealing in some manner, with horses and cattle. If red, he will find much distinction in some area of military life should he decide to pursue this. But, if somewhat raised and reddish toned, it shows much good fortune, usually in something related to fires.

A mole that appears on the right side of the forehead, on the line of the Sun, shows that another will be found on the right breast. A woman possessing such a mole will have an affluent life, but she will also, if the mole is black, have to be extremely subservient to her lovers, or her husband.

Appearing on a man, such moles signify general good fortune in all aspects of life, some riches, and many honors. But should this mole be black, everything will be the result of the efforts of friends rather than from his own merits.

A mole appearing on the left side of the forehead, on the line of the Moon, denotes that another will also be located on the left breast. When this is seen on a woman, it signifies that she will find many lovers in a social level far above her own.

Such a mole appearing on a man denotes a jealous, very covetous nature. If red, he will be rash, and if black, evil intentioned and totally untrustworthy. Yellow or purple moles in this area denote cleverness, but a life checkered with serious problems, most of these being the result of amorous advances.

A mole appearing between the eyebrows, or on the line of *Venus*, denotes that another is to be found directly under the belly button or the navel. On a woman, it signifies more than one marriage due to her husband's untimely death. Three or more marriages are seen if the mole is black.

When this same mole is found on a man, and it is red in color, he will acquire a large fortune through his wife. If brownish, he will lose both his wife and his finances. But should the mole be purple or even black, prosperity will be his whether he marries or not.

When a mole develops on the nose itself, in the area assigned to Mercury, it also signifies that a mole will be found somewhere in the genital region of the individual. A woman possessing such a mole will be extremely passionate, but she will marry and try very hard to be completely faithful to her husband.

This same mole found on a man also indicates a sensuous nature, but one that can be satisfied through a good marriage. He though, is more apt to search out other companions to alleviate these strong urges, and will be quite adaptable to a variety of partners.

BOOK IV
CONCERNING MOLES
ON THE BODY

Moles are said to be indications of a person's character and, supposedly, are the result of occult planetary influences. A round mole signifies good; an oblong one, a mixture of good and evil; and an angular mole denotes misfortune. Hairy moles signify evil tidings, as does a dark mole. The significations of many moles according to the ancient teachings of the gypsies are as arranged below.

A mole on the lower part of the neck on the right side near the shoulder, indicates a man who is extremely greedy. On a female it denotes that she will be loved by someone far above her social standing.

A mole in the same area, but near the left shoulder, tells of either sex falling into disgrace through evil practices.

A mole on the left shoulder predicts that the man will have many financial problems. It shows that a woman will have a life full of anxiety and humiliation brought on by her own vanity. If this mole is dark colored or black, her conduct will bring about disgrace and ruin of reputation.

A mole on the right shoulder shows that a man will experience good fortune in all of his undertakings. If it happens to be red hued, then he will share a large fortune with his wife or lover. If a woman has this same mole on her right shoulder, it denotes that she is to wed above her expectations. If dark, or black in color, she will bury her first husband and remarry.

A mole in the center of the throat, that is on the gullet, indicates much danger in the life of a man. He may face death by hanging or through strangulation, accidental or otherwise. On the throat of a woman, she will face great peril with an illness, and if it happens to be black, she may even die.

A mole on the left side of the throat signifies that a man may experience a dangerous fall from a horse, or from a high building. It denotes the same thing for a woman and, if the mole is pale in color, danger by water.

A mole on the right side of the throat shows a man with a great sense of humor, but a very short life-span. For a woman, this same mole denotes a reasonably blissful life, but extreme danger and pain during childbirth.

A mole at the nape of the neck tells either a man or a woman of great danger and of untimely death, probably by water.

A mole immediately under the left breast denotes a man of a hateful nature, and with a furious temper, but strong in feelings of love and devotion. On a woman, it shows that she is always faithful and considerate, and that this fidelity will make her suffer eternally.

A mole immediately under the right breast shows a man that will be extremely lucky in pursuing a career in agriculture. A woman possessing this same mole shall receive an inheritance from someone who has recently died. If this mole happens to be very dark, or black in color, her father will be killed in an unfortunate accident.

A mole on the genitals of a man indicates that he will be extremely passionate, and fond of luxurious living. His life will be enriched by marriage. A woman possessing this very same mole is rather sensuous, and although it will be difficult, she will try her best to remain faithful to her husband.

A mole on either the left or the right knee, is a prediction of long journeys for both sexes. Such people are destined to be married only for the sake of convenience, and then probably to a foreigner. They usually make fortunate matches.

A mole on the calf of the right leg indicates that a man will gain a high position and honors by his own ingenuity. If the mole is dark, he will suffer much unhappiness due to his involvements with a variety of women. But, should this mole appear to be raised, he will marry a loving person, be faithful to her, and live a long life filled with happy moments. If this same mole is found on the calf of a woman, she is destined to marry someone who is wealthy, and she will bear many children and live long.

A mole on the right foot of a man indicates that he will be most clever, will learn foreign languages easily, and will be an intelligent student of the occult. To a woman, this same mole promises a fortune-filled, happy, and long life. If this mole happens to be dark colored, or black, she will experience quite a few troubles along the road of life.

A mole on the left foot of a man denotes that he will be rash in important matters, and he will possess an evil disposition. To a woman, this same mole signifies many problems, a life full of anxiety, and troubles throughout her life. If the mole happens to be black, she can expect much danger when traveling, and a multitude of narrow escapes in business dealings.

If the second toe on either foot has a mole growing on it, it denotes a happy and prosperous life, and riches. If the mole is dark, it signifies great losses of money.

BOOK V
CORRESPONDING MOLES
on the face
and body

Ancient astrologers determined that when a mole was found on the face of a person, a corresponding mole would normally also be developed on some specific part of the body. These dual moles had particular meanings attached to them:

A person with a mole near the right ear, will have another mole on the right side of the stomach. This mole signifies that a man will suffer from a blow to the head, which in turn will cause an accidental injury to his ear. He may lose his hearing. If this mole happens to be black in color, these evils will be even more disastrous. On a woman, it indicates the loss of everything she values.

A mole on or near the left ear, indicates that the person will have a corresponding mole located in a lower position on the belly. This mole signifies persecution of a man by his enemies. If it happens to be of red hue, he will come close to committing murder for a woman. If black in color, or even honey-colored, it is still extremely evil in connotation, and he will have many quarrels and possibly face a violent death. If a woman possesses this identical mole, whatever the color, it shows that she will be the main cause of someone's death. She should be left alone to meddle with her own poison and all men should shun her evil intentions.

A mole on the right cheek points to the existence of another on the right hip. On a man, this signifies that he will have great charm for the opposite sex, and women will flock to him in droves. The color has no bearing in this case. A woman with the same two moles will find happiness in marriage, and will be beloved deeply by her spouse.

A mole on the left cheek shows that there will be another on the left hip. This indicates, on a man, that he will experience a wandering existence and a relatively short life. If it happens to be black, he will die from unexpected violence. On a woman, the same two corresponding moles signify a threat to her happiness, misfortune in financial matters, and general grief throughout life.

A mole on the right corner of the mouth signifies that another can be found at the right side of the lower part of the spine. It indicates, to a man, that he will accumulate a great deal of wealth through his own shrewdness. But, if this mole is honey-colored, his great wealth and good fortune will come from a woman. On a woman, the same two moles tell that she will abound in wealth, and will be dearly loved by her mate. If these moles happen to be black in color, she will suffer from the scandal created by other envious women. Her wealth cannot prevent this.

A mole on the left side of the mouth indicates that there will be another found on the left side of the spinal base. On a man, this shows that he will become seriously entangled with a woman he cannot possibly marry and make respectable. She will bear him more than one illegitimate child. On a woman, these moles show that she will, in all likelihood, suffer from this same disgrace. Let this be a fair warning to those with these signs.

When a mole appears in the middle of the upper lip, another can readily be found around the genital area, in both sexes. On a man, this is an indication that he will be miserable from many and various perils. Women will be his downfall. To a woman, these same two moles tell that she will suffer illnesses, and will be weak with internal diseases.

A mole beneath the middle of the upper lip shows that another can be found on the knee. This indicates, on a man, that he is destined to take many long and tedious journeys. He will visit many foreign lands and see strange things. If the mole is honey-colored, he will surely gain great wealth from strangers, and eventually marry a rich, foreign woman. This same set of moles show a woman to be thoughtless. She, too, will marry a foreigner and live most of her life out of her own country. She will not be happy in this union, but will stick it out for the money.

A mole upon the middle of the chin shows that another can be found upon the right foot. On a man, this indicates that he will experience nothing but good fortune through a variety of women friends. To a woman, these same moles signify a happy marital union, but many worries with her children. Although pleased with her marriage, she is liable to be unfaithful because of some lack in self-control.

A mole on the right side of the chin indicates that another may be found on the right haunch. These moles signify that a man will be of great intellectual capacity. If the moles are black in color, he will research in the occult realm. In a woman, these moles show extremely good fortune, a happy marriage, and a long and fruitful life. The color matters not here.

A mole on the left side of the chin will have a corresponding mole on the left haunch. To a man, this indicates that he will have misfortune as well as good luck, much anxiety, bodily discomfort, and mental anguish. In a woman, it tells of ill health and, if of a pale-bluish color, danger while traveling.

BOOK VI
ancient secrets of
craniology

One of the first essays ever written on the subject of craniology, was by the most famous of all Greek physicians, Hippocrates (460 B.C. - 357 B.C.). Known today as the "father of
medicine," this learned and knowing man left us a treatise
which covered the various forms of the head and their particular
indications. His writing encompassed highlights of what he
called craniology, but what we recognize today as parts of both
phrenology and physiognomy.

In his sixth book, which concerned ordinary diseases, Hippocrates wrote that by considering the head of a man, the
whole body may be accurately judged. His reasoning was that
since the head is the most apparent part of the body in that it is
not covered or masked, this area is most suitable of all for
determining the temperament and the actions of a person. This
great scholar placed much of his emphasis upon the facial

characteristics, as well as the form, proportion, and dimensions of the head. He believed that a combination of all these things would enable man accurately to judge the mind of another, such mind being the only thing that distinguished us from the beasts.

It is not infrequently claimed today that physiognomy, as a science, only dates from the eighteenth century, and that it was first reduced to a system by Johann Kaspar Lavater (1741-1801), a celebrated Swiss mystic. He was a poet, pastor, and physiognomist in his day. Thus, Lavater's name is generally associated with this ancient science, often mistakenly, as its originator. He published *Physiognomical Fragments,* a four-volume work, between 1775 and 1778, which was translated into English in London, in 1789.

Phrenology, on the other hand, is most often said to be the brainchild of Dr. Joseph Franz Gall (1758-1828), a practicing physician in Vienna. This respected doctor made extensive comparisons of the skulls of man and animals, and subsequently assigned specific locations to twenty major organs in the head, organs that determined the basic characteristics of every human being. He is credited with assigning the proper classifications and nomenclature to the science of phrenology.

But, the truth is that physiognomy, and to some extent phrenology, were studied and practiced in connection with astrology for ages before either of the above men were even born. Then referred to as craniology, these sciences had a much more comprehensive meaning than do the more modern definitions. To use the words of one ancient writer:

> It was a craft whereby the conditions of men and their temperaments were fully known by the lineaments and conjectures of their faces. It consisted of two things, the complexion and the composition of the face and body of man; both of which do manifestly declare and show the things that are within the man, by the external signs; as by the color, the stature, the composition and the shape of the members.

Lavater did not invent physiognomy any more than Dr. Gall invented phrenology. These men merely attempted to divorce these studies from what they considered to be the occult sciences. Instead of leaving physiognomy and phrenology under the government of those immutable laws which control the motions of the stars, they both framed a set of arbitrary rules, founded upon the suggestions of their fancies, and then proceeded to apply their rules in all cases with as much confidence as if they had been based upon the experience of centuries. The fallability, or to be a little more blunt, the absurdity of these fanciful rules has been demonstrated in innumerable instances, and the physiognomy of Lavater as well as the phrenology of Dr. Gall have long since fallen into disrepute.

But, the original science of craniology which these two men so mutilated and garbled, is, in its integrity, as a part and portion of celestial philosophy, as true now as it was in the days of the great Hippocrates and his multitude of followers. Hippocrates sincerely believed that the innermost part of the soul could be truly discerned by means of craniology, and he wrote that Socrates himself (469 B.C. - 399 B.C.), the most virtuous of philosophers, was lustful, obscene, and luxurious by nature. Socrates readily admitted that this description was entirely correct, and went on to declare that it was only by the stern and watchful exercise of his reason, that he had been able to keep his vicious propensities in check, and thereby prevent himself from committing a thousand abominations.

Even Homer, the Greek epic poet who flourished long before any of the above men, sometime between 950 and 850 B.C., included some elements of what was later to be known as craniology, in his various writings. For example, in the *Iliad* he describes Thersites and Irus as evil speakers, and notes the following outward and visible signs of the malicious disposition of one of them:

> It seemed here that Nature needs would be
> Employed to forge out all deformity;
> He was purblind, cramp-shouldered too, and lame,
> Sharp head and ill-boned body out of frame;
> But little hair, and long and folio ear,
> In brief, so ugly as to kindle fear.

Figure 13

Socrates (469 B.C. *-399* B.C. *), a great philosopher whom Hippocrates called lustful, obscene, and luxurious by nature—a revelation determined by the manner in which his head was shaped.*

We know too, that craniology was commonly practiced by the Hebrews and, in fact, the Old Testament gives us splendid examples of the craniology of Moses, Jacob, David, Jonathan, Absalom and many others. The compilers of the Jewish Talmud bequeathed a treatise on this subject to the world, which included the innermost thoughts of both the sacred and the profane writers of the early ages. This very old manuscript is more in conjunction with the ageless science of metoposcopy (Book II), which more pointedly refers to the forehead of man, and the planetary lines which are to be found upon it.

Hippocrates himself assigned certain planets, as well as the signs of the zodiac, to various parts of the face. These were accepted without question by the Greeks, Romans, and the Hebrews of that day and age. They were ordained and constituted as follows:

Mars . . . . Forehead
Sun or Sol . . . . Right eye
Moon or Luna . . . . Left eye

Jupiter . . . . Right ear
Saturn . . . . Left ear
Venus . . . . .Nose
Mercury . . . . Mouth

Cancer . . . . Zenith of the forehead
Taurus . . . . .Middle of the forehead
Leo . . . . Right eyebrow
Aquarius . . . . Left eyebrow
Sagittarius . . . . Right eye
Gemini . . . . Left eye
Libra . . . . Right ear
Aries . . . . Left ear
Scorpio . . . . .Nose
Virgo . . . . Right cheek
Pisces . . . . Left cheek
Capricorn . . . . Lowest point on chin

In Hippocrates' works, we find that he believed a little head never to be without vice and, most commonly, to be guilty of little wisdom. It is instead, full of folly, which is often malicious. A very large head was said usually to signify a good-natured person, but one with few, if any manners. The most perfectly shaped head is considered to be a round one, which is somewhat depressed on both sides. The best size was found to be moderate, or in-between the small and the very large, and containing a small depression in the back part.

The human brain was considered to be one of the noblest parts of the body, and its formation was determined by the outward appearance of the cranium. If the head was "corrupted," or of an odd size and shape, then the brain was said also to be warped. The head of a man was believed to have proportionately more brains than all other living creatures, and more brains than women.

So, the well-formed head should be shaped like a mallet or a sphere with some clear high points both before and behind, and it should especially have a high point or bulge in its center portion.

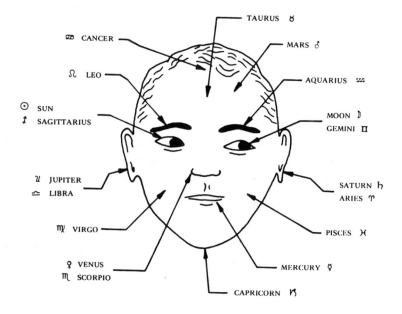

Figure 14

The signs of the zodiac and of the planets assigned to the various parts of the face, by Hippocrates himself.

If the front part of a head shows a depression or cavity, the person is said to possess little or no good judgment. If a cavity appears in the back of the head, he will have no memory, and will be rather slow moving and weak, physically.

The strength of the human brain was thought to be demonstrated by the strength of the body and the nerves, and also by the breadth of the shoulders, the chest, and the arms and legs. The head which is of a handsome and decent form increases the virtues and intensifies the senses of a person, and denotes integrity, honor, and magnificence of character. The head that appears to be deformed in any manner signifies exactly the opposite of the above qualities.

A big head with a very broad forehead denotes, according to Hippocrates, a man who is slow acting and rather gentle, yet one who is industrious and far from lazy.

A head that appears to be low and flat signifies impudence and lustfulness. Such persons have loose morals, and are lewd in their thinking, as well as wanton in their actions. A high and flat head denotes much foolishness, and a general appearance of stupidity.

When a man or a woman has a very long and pointed head, it signifies that they are gluttons about food, as well as being very rash in their actions. They are shameless people who are bold and vivacious in youth, but through excessiveness, lose their vitality. Many such heads can be seen among us.

When the head is very large in proportion to the rest of the body, and the sinews of the neck are big and very strong, it is a sign of strength and courage. These individuals have a temper and are inclined to anger rather easily, yet they are honorable.

When the head appears to be extremely large, and way out of proportion to the body, the person will be of a foolish nature, quite shiftless or lazy, and not far from madness. They seldom do anything that would indicate class or good breeding, but instead seem to live in perpetual sadness and gloom.

A head which is well-shaped, and balanced in proportion to the body, signifies a great deal of wisdom and goodness. This is even more true when the front of the forehead is well developed.

When the front of the head bulges at the sides, it denotes a rational, comprehensive thinking pattern, eloquence, and a strong desire to learn and know things.

A head that appears to be altogether globe-shaped, signifies one who is always on the move, fickle, and forgetful. Such people practice little discretion, and possess very little wisdom.

A head that appears to be very long, horizontally, and slanting, or on an incline, denotes insolence, disrespect, and impertinence. Such people are indiscreet and unwise. They wear themselves out by taking part in corrupt and dishonorable sexual activities.

A head that appears to be dented in the rear in a ditchlike formation, or a depressed hollow, denotes a person who is controlled by fits of anger and an uncontrollable temper. These individuals are usually depressed in spirit and have a gloomy outlook.

Aristotle (384 B.C.-322 B.C.), a very distinguished philosopher and naturalist of ancient Greece, studied in the school of Plato. He was a prolific writer who, accordingly, had much to say in regard to craniology, stressing in this instance the various forms of the forehead. A square forehead, he said, denotes the high-minded, honorable person: *Quadrata frons pro faciei ratione mediocris magnanimos ostendit ob similitudinem leonis.* Those possessing such a forehead are as courageous as the lion, and are compared to these beasts because of their strength, courage, and sense of judgment.

The concave forehead, which contains pits and bumps or mounts, is a certain sign of deceitfulness, a liar, ambition, and fearlessness.

A clear forehead, without wrinkles, signifies a malicious disposition which is truly devoted to little good. Such people like to debate and argue over almost any issue.

He that is bald, or has a little hair growing on the forepart of the head, but none on the forehead itself, and with delicate, smooth-appearing skin, is full of wrath, inconsistent, and in bad physical shape.

He that has a forehead that appears to be gathered together and full of wrinkles, is noted as a flatterer, and is said to have the nature of a dog, for flattery is used to deceive others.

Aspera fronte ne gaudeas, neque fossas monticulos habeat; omnia namque haec signa versutiam et infidelitatem nunciant, et interdum stultitiam et insanium: He that has a frowning, wrinkled forehead is of a gloomy disposition, is usually depressed and dejected, and thinks more than he speaks. Everything is carefully thought out before a word is spoken. These people are gentle, good conversationalists, and even more melancholy if wealthy.

The little forehead denotes the person who is lazy, wicked and inclined to mischief. They believe nothing but their own foolish opinions, and are to be compared among the beasts to the cat or rat. They are also an epitome of cruelty and cowardice.

The very broad forehead represents a person who is gluttonous and unclean in sexual matters, being somewhat the nature of the swine. Such persons use flattery to win others in friendship, but they are enemies behind a man's back. They lie, and speak offensively about those they pretend to feel friendship and affection for.

A forehead that appears to be pointed at the temples, so the bones seem to be almost fleshless, signifies great vanity, changeableness, and little capacity or determination for business endeavors.

A cloudy forehead, or one full of black marks, is a sign of boldness. Such people are likened to bulls and lions who are perpetually angry or throwing a fit of temper.

A forehead that is neither straight nor crooked, fat nor lean, smooth nor rough, but between all of these things, signifies a well-rounded personality, and the individual who is devoid of trickery and deceit in his friendships.

Epicurus (342 B.C. - 270 B.C.), another well-known Greek philosopher, was also intensely interested in craniology, and he, too, left posterity with some thoughts on this subject. This great man had numerous disciples in both Greece and Rome, and although he was a voluminous writer, but very few of his numerous manuscripts are extant today.

A very large and spacious forehead denotes a sluggish and fearful person. Most people possessing such a forehead are honorable, and they do not take advantage of others.

A forehead that is broad on all sides, without hair, or as it were, bald, reveals a courageous, sometimes insolent person, but also one with a great degree of understanding. Yet, these same individuals can be malicious, easily angered, dishonest, and liars when it is felt to be necessary.

Those who have flesh around the eyes, so that the eyebrows hang down like those of hounds, are fraudulent, cruel, and unmerciful. They are also very bold, untiring, and willing to fight whenever they feel the need to do so.

A depressed and low forehead denotes an effeminate person. This type of forehead suits a woman, but when a man possesses it, he will be low in spirits, and a cringing soul. He is fearful, submissive and feminine in actions, a person who is easily swayed or convinced by the words of even the most simple-minded man that he is afraid of.

The very small head is always a sign of evil, for the smaller it is, the more foolish its owner will be. These people will experience much illness because of the small quantity of their brains. A head of this size, according to Epicurus, jumbles and smothers the brains, which, in turn, creates a lack of memory. Such a person is short of temper, hasty in actions, always on the move, and will not exceed fifty-six years of age.

A pleasantly shaped, normal-size head denotes those who are wise, in good physical condition, studious, and avid readers.

A forehead that appears to be severe and stern at first sight, indicates a strange, uncivilized, savage disposition which is prone to all types of cruelty. Such people know no pity, especially if they also happen to be depressed in spirits.

A forehead that appears to be low in the middle, and wrinkled so its possessor seems to frown, denotes a person of simple tastes, and one who is brave in the face of adversity. Fortune is often very cruel to these people.

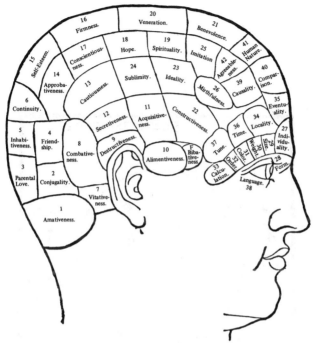

NAMES, NUMBERING, AND DEFINITIONS OF THE FACULTIES.

1. AMATIVENESS.—Sexual love, fondness, passion.
2. CONJUGALITY.—The pairing instinct, one love.
3. PARENTAL LOVE.—Care for offspring, and young.
4. FRIENDSHIP.—Sociability, clinging to friends.
5. INHABITIVENESS.—Love of home, patriotism.
6. CONTINUITY.—Application, finishing, continuing.
7. VITATIVENESS.—Clinging to life, resisting disease.
8. COMBATIVENESS.—Defense, courage, force, etc.
9. DESTRUCTIVENESS.—Executiveness, severity.
10. ALIMENTIVENESS.—Appetite, relish, greediness.
11. ACQUISITIVENESS.—Frugality, saving, industry.
12. SECRETIVENESS.—Self-control, policy, art, tact.
13. CAUTIOUSNESS.—Guardedness, safety, prudence.
14. APPROBATIVENESS.—Pride of character, honor.
15. SELF-ESTEEM.—Self-respect, dignity, authority.
16. FIRMNESS.—Stability, perseverance, willfulness.
17. CONSCIENTIOUSNESS.—Duty, right, truth, justice.
18. HOPE.—Expectation, anticipation, enterprise.
19. SPIRITUALITY.—Intuition, prescience, faith.
20. VENERATION.—Worship, adoration, obedience.
21. BENEVOLENCE.—Sympathy, kindness, goodness.

22. CONSTRUCTIVENESS.—Ingenuity, invention.
23. IDEALITY.—*Taste*, love of beauty, poetry.
24. SUBLIMITY.—Love of grandeur, vastness, etc.
25. IMITATION.—Copying, aptitude, mimickry.
26. MIRTH.—Fun, wit, ridicule, facetiousness.
27. INDIVIDUALITY.—Observation, desire to *see*.
28. FORM.—Memory of *shape*, looks, persons.
29. SIZE.—Measurement of quantity, distance.
30. WEIGHT.—Control of motion, balancing.
31. COLOR.—Discernment and love of colors.
32. ORDER.—*Method*, system, doing by *rule*.
33. CALCULATION.—Mental arithmetic, reckoning.
34. LOCALITY.—Memory of place, position, etc.
35. EVENTUALITY.—Memory of facts, events, etc.
36. TIME.—Telling *when*, time of day, dates, etc.
37. TUNE.—Musical love, ecstacy, and talent.
38. LANGUAGE—*Expression* by words, acts, etc.
39. CAUSALITY.—*Planning*, thinking, reason, sense.
40. COMPARISON.—Analysis, inferring, critic.
41. HUMAN NATURE.—Perception of character.
42. SUAVITY.—*Pleasantness*, blandness, blarney.

Figure 15

This illustration appeared in The Practical Phrenologist, *by O. S. Fowler, published in 1869. It reflects the version of craniology developed by Dr. Gall in 1791, in which each area of the skull so marked, represents either a bump or a depression. Through a check of a person's head, the various character traits were said to be accurately determined in any individual.*

Figure 16

Phrenology and astrology teach many of the same things in a somewhat different manner. The phrenologist utilizes measurements of the head to show where the various functions lie. The astrologist utilizes the zodiac to show where the greatest influence lies that put the bumps or functions where they are in the first place.

If the forehead appears to be swollen because of the abundant flesh at the temples, or if the cheeks and jaws are fleshy and full, great courage and a willingness to fight is evident. These people make the best soldiers because they are proud, they anger easily, and they are always ready to engage in combat.

BOOK VII
astrological pharmacy
or the secrets
of medicinal herbs

The ancient mystics who wrote on astrology, magic, and forms of divination give voluminous directions for gathering herbs and plants at certain periods during the waxing and waning of the moon. The more modern practitioners of the mystical arts, for the most part reject many of these formulas. Instead, they rely rather upon the nature of the plants themselves, and upon the predominating stellar influences that are in full force at the time the plant juices are extracted and prepared for medicinal use. The time of harvest, and the moment of juice extraction are believed to be the two most important things necessary to produce the intended effects of the various vegetable medicines used in astrological pharmacy.

A French astrologer privately published an occult work in 1582. In this book, he insists that any plant bearing a resemblance to a portion of the human frame, is specifically designed by nature to cure or alleviate the suffering of the member it resembles from disease. This astrologer of the past gives a number of illustrations, a few of which, modernized from the quaint and somewhat coarse language of the book, are cited below. How far the actual facts will bear out the doctrine of affinities laid down by that author, the reader can ascertain only through experimentation, or through concentrated research.

When a certain plant resembles the nose in its configuration, as do the leaves of the wild-water mint, they are extremely beneficial in restoring the sense of smell.

Herbs and seeds, when shaped like teeth, such as the tooth-wort or the pine kernel, etc., are said to preserve the dental organization.

Plants resembling the figure of the heart are comforting to that organ. Therefore, the Fuller's thistle, balm, mint, parsley, citron-apple, white-beet, spikenard, and motherwort, which bear in leaves and roots a heartlike form, are congenial to that organ.

Shrubs and herbs similar in shape to the bladder, are said to be excellent for those parts. These would include nightshade, nux visicaria and the alkekengi, for they all relieve the organ of stones.

Walnuts, Indian nuts, leeks, and the ragwort root, because of their basic form, and when properly prepared, are said to further generation and prevent sterility in man and woman.

Fleshy plants make flesh for their consumers; for instance, the onion, leek and colewort are said to do this.

Herbs which tend to be rather milky in their substance are said to foster the production of milk, especially during mother-hood. Lettuce and the fruit of the almond and fig trees are especially adaptable.

Plants that are hollow, as the stalks of grain, reeds, leeks, garlic, etc., are excellent for purging, opening, and soothing the hollow parts of the body.

Certain plants are said to fortify and brace the nerves. For example, nettles, the roots of the mallotus, the herb neuras, the sensitive plant, etc., are said to be ideal medicines. These may also be used as external applications.

Herbs whose acidity turns milk to curd, are said to lead to procreation. Such are gallium, and the seeds of spurge.

Vegetables that tend to be shaped like ears, as the leaves of the folefoot or the wild spikenard, are said to improve both the hearing faculties and the memory when correctly prepared and eaten. Another wonderful cure for deafness, this one nonvegetarian but, nevertheless, worth mentioning here, is the oil that is extracted from the shells of sea-snails.

Plants that are shaped like the liver, such as the liverwort, figs, trinity, fermitory and agaric, are efficacious in assisting in the cure of all bilious disorders and diseases.

Oily vegetable products such as the filbert, walnut, almond, peanut, etc., are excellent for those who wish to gain weight.

Plants that appear to be naturally lean tend to emaciate those who use them regularly. These include such things as the long-leaved rosa solis and the sarsaparilla.

Certain plants, having a resemblance to the womb, such as the birthwort, ladie's seal, bryony, and heartwort, etc., assist in bringing about a safe natural birth.

Plants of knobbed form, like the knuckles or joints of man, are said to be excellent for spinal complaints, kidney disease, knee swellings, foot gout, and all diseases causing pains in the joints. These plants would include galingales and the knotty odoriferous rush (calami).

Maidenhair and the moss of quinces resemble the fibers of the head. Therefore a mixture of these items are said to be very good for curing baldness.

Herbs that simulate the shape of the lungs, such as lungwort, hound's-tongue, sage, and camphrey, are said to be good for every type of pulmonary complaint.

Herbs formed somewhat like the spleen are recommended for strengthening that part of the anatomy. These include such plants as the miltwort, lupine and the spleenwort.

Another, later, astrologer produced more natural home remedies, but these do not necessarily require the plant, root, or bark to resemble the organ of the body in order to be effective. Rather than gather these various items in accordance with the position of the moon, he states that the following rules will bring satisfactory results:

1. Flowers should be gathered when they first begin to blossom and no later.

2. Leaves must be gathered and collected only just before they fade in the autumn.

3. Herbs the same as above.

4. Seeds are to be collected just before ripening.

5. Barks should be gathered as soon as they will easily peel off in the early spring, but no later.

6. Roots may be dug up at any time, thoroughly washed, dried, and carefully stored in a dark place.

Vegetables

Raw onions: When sliced and set around on plates, will absorb contagion in the air. If many are eaten prior to entering an infected area, the person will be safeguarded against all diseases.

Potato: For good results a scraped potato should be carefully placed upon an area of the skin that has been burned.

Garlic: May be utilized as an external application, or made into a syrup by crushing, and is said to be excellent in curing colds, asthma, and coughs.

Miscellaneous vegetable remedies: Spinach is said to have a direct effect upon kidney complaints, as does the common dandelion when used as greens. Asparagus purifies the blood, while celery acts admirably upon the central nervous system and is said to be a certain cure for rheumatism and neuralgia. Tomatoes act upon the liver, while beets and turnips stimulate the appetite. Lettuce and cucumbers have an overall cooling effect on the system, and the bean is a strengthening vegetable. Onions, garlic, leeks, chives, and shallots, all of which are similar, stimulate the circulatory system and promote good digestion. Red onions are an excellent diuretic, and white ones are recommended eaten raw as a remedy for insomnia. They are also a nutritious tonic, for in a soup, they restore strength to the digestive organs.

Bark

American poplar: The inner bark of this tree should be dried and then powdered. Taken by the teaspoonful, three or four times a day, is said to relieve chronic rheumatism.

Dogwood: A handful of this bark should be boiled in a quart of ordinary water. A wineglass of this strong tealike mixture is said to bring down fevers and relieve chills.

Oak bark: A tea made from oak bark is supposed to relieve a fever, and rubbed on externally, it is good for healing sores. When the acorns are roasted and eaten, they are said to cure various skin diseases.

Peach-tree bark: Three wineglasses of a tea made from this bark acts as a sedative and stops vomiting and nausea.

Willow: The bark of this tree is said to have properties, if taken as a strong tea, that will bring down fevers.

Wild cherry: The inner bark of the roots and the berries of this tree, dried and powdered, is said to cure palpitation of the heart, a poor appetite, bad digestion, and nervousness. One heaping teaspoonful should be left in cold water for at least twenty-four hours before using. A glass should be taken four times daily.

Roots

Blackberry roots: This root is said to be an excellent remedy for diarrhea if boiled in a quart of water until it thickens and taken by the tablespoon, three times daily.

Burdock root: A handful of the freshly gathered root is to be boiled in a quart of water until it is half gone. Drinking a pint a day is said to be one of the best remedies for skin diseases.

Dandelion root: Best collected in July or August, its fluid is recommended for liver problems, constipation, and coughs.

Horseradish root: This root is boiled down to a syrup, and two teaspoonfuls taken twice daily. It is said to cure palsy, rheumatism, and hoarseness.

Mandrake or Mayapple root: This root is dried and powdered, and taken as is. It is said to be a stimulant, tonic, and laxative, and it is good for various liver complaints.

Leaves and Berries

Black elder: The flowers and berries both possess medicinal properties. The flowers, when stirred into fresh melted lard and then strained, make excellent paste for applying to burns, scalds, wounds and nonhealing sores. The berries, when eaten, act as a mild laxative, and are said to be good also for skin diseases and as a rheumatism cure.

Boneset or thoroughwort: The leaves and flowers are made into a strong tea which is said to be a good rejuvenating tonic; helpful when chills and fever strike.

Flaxseed: The seeds should be placed in a linen bag and suspended in a dish of water. After soaking for several hours, the tea will be ready to drink. It is said to be excellent for colds, coughs, and disorders of the bowels, kidneys, and the bladder.

Juniper: The berries of the juniper tree should be thoroughly crushed, breaking all of the seeds. Two teaspoonsful daily, dried or fresh, is said to help cure skin problems and dropsy.

Herbal Teas

Herbal teas are said to serve as preventatives or outright cures for innumerable illnesses. Some of these unusual treatments are described herein. The juice of the sage plant, added to water and taken as a tea is supposed to settle the stomach, and be an excellent remedy for colds. Sage tea, sweetened with honey is said to be unusually good for gargling to relieve a sore throat. Hop tea produces pleasant relaxing sleep, and may also be applied externally to bruises and sprains for quick relief. Catnip tea, as well as most others, are made simply by infusing the dried and green leaves and stalks in boiling water, letting them stand until cold, and then sweetening to taste. The catnip variety of tea is said to be excellent for infant colds, as is pennyroyal tea. Camomile tea is an excellent all-around tonic. Tea made from blackberry roots, as well as that from green strawberry leaves, is a soothing wash for a cankered mouth. Mint tea, made from the green leaves, is a healing agent for the stomach and the bowels.

Fruit

Lemons are thought by many to be one of man's greatest blessings, because of their healthful and curative qualities. A person afflicted with dropsy can supposedly cure himself by eating lemons. He is told to start by eating one lemon a day, and continually to increase his intake until he is eating ten to fifteen a day.

If a throbbing headache strikes, drink the pure juice of half a lemon. Then drink the juice from the other half within the next thirty minutes. Meanwhile, a slice of lemon should be rubbed over the brow and temples. This procedure, it is said, will make the headache pain go away.

If complexion problems are evident, and freckles disliked, simply squeeze the juice of a lemon into a glass of milk. Rub this preparation over the face and neck, and leave it there overnight. The skin will glow and the freckles will have disappeared by the next morning.

Dazzling white hands are readily obtainable by rubbing lemon juice mixed with glycerine onto the hands, and then wearing gloves to bed.

Lemon juice is said to be a sure cure for mosquito or other insect bites. Simply touch the spot with pure lemon juice, and all the sting and itching will disappear.

Corns and warts are said to be eliminated by binding a piece of lemon on them for a few days. It softens the growth so that it can easily be removed.

If your hair is falling out, rub slices of lemon thoroughly into the roots and over the entire scalp, washing afterwards with warm, soapy water. It is said to be a sure cure for dandruff, as well as a hair-root strengthener.

Lemon taken before meals is said to be advantageous as a certain preventative and cure for heartburn.

The juice of a lemon, taken in a little warm water just before retiring, has been said to prove beneficial in relieving the most obstinate cases of rheumatism and gout. Very hot lemon juice taken in this manner breaks up a cold, and is said to cure a sore throat.

To overcome a tired feeling, and when the bones seem to ache, lemon juice squeezed into fresh water, enough to make a sour beverage, will make a person feel refreshed if taken freely many times a day. It will also sweeten a sour stomach.

Even seasickness, a problem of many travelers, is said to be avoided by taking the juice of one lemon each morning before breakfast, in pure water, for one week before going aboard ship.

BOOK VIII
the mysterious
wheel of astrology

A unique method of divination, using the Golden Wheel, will accurately answer the following questions for those who query it sincerely:

1. Will I recover from an illness?
2. Will I obtain the favor I wish for from a certain person?
3. Will I get the advancement or promotion I want?
4. Shall I marry or shall I not marry?
5. Will I become rich, poor, or what?
6. Will a certain friendship be advantageous?
7. Will my expectations or wishes come true?
8. Will an illness be of long or short duration?

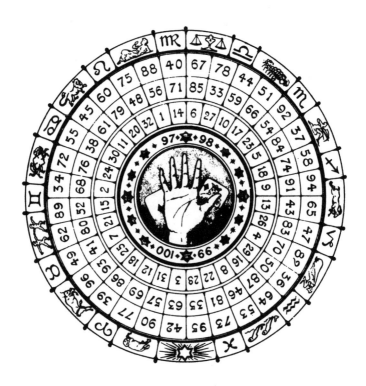

Figure 17

This Golden Wheel was extremely popular as a method of divination during the Middle Ages, and is said to have been regularly utilized by Cagliostro, a celebrated mystic, during the latter part of the eighteenth century. This Golden Wheel was formerly included in an old Latin manuscript on astrology, and translated into English by a seer of the late eighteen hundreds.

How to Use the Golden Wheel

The person who desires to have his fortune told must first take the Golden Wheel and place it face down on a table. Shut the eyes tightly and proceed to prick into a number with a pointed instrument. Then turn the wheel over and determine which number was selected by the hand of fate. Now, refer to the Table of Futurity and find the answer or explanation corresponding to the number you pricked.

Table of Futurity

The following will be the correct answers for either sex. The individual using this wheel must, therefore, specify whether the question is personal or for his or her mate. The answers may also be altered to fit from husband to wife, or wife to husband, etc.

1. The querent will certainly marry into wealth, but the mate will be extremely homely.

2. Someone who is absent at present will soon return. Do not follow through with present plans.

3. Shows legal problems, financial losses, infidelity in love matters, unsuccessful ventures, and friendship loss.

4. Any extravagant desire will not be granted. Be cautious as to how money is spent.

5. Excellent luck is in store. Sudden prosperity. Great respect from prominent people. An important letter to arrive soon.

6. A letter of abuse can soon be expected. Try to collect all outstanding debts from both friends and acquaintances.

7. Your lover will be scrupulously honest and faithful. An outsider will try to disrupt this.

8. A friend will soon return from a long trip. You will benefit immensely from his wealth.

9. You are destined to find a loving partner; success in all undertakings; a large and prosperous family.

10. Your mate will not make a great fortune. Your assistance will bring a high standard of living. You will not be poor by any stretch of the imagination.

11. You are destined to take a sudden, unexpected trip. A pleasant individual will accompany you on this trip. Your family will eventually benefit from this.

12. You may be able to regain all that has been lost, but it will take determination, perseverance, and trouble.

13. An unexpected letter of grave importance is due to arrive. A relative will soon die. You will inherit a great deal of money.

14. You will make great financial and social gains if you advance with caution. You will suffer great discomfort.

15. You will eventually be comfortably settled, but you will bear many crosses on the way up in the world.

16. Persevere and you will gain a great unexpected advantage. A sudden acquaintance with one of the opposite sex is about to take place. Be on guard against trickery.

17. You will have an agreeable partner for life. He or she will have little or no temper. A large family of children is in store for you.

18. Let the one who selects this number persevere, for the ideas and plans are excellent and must be successful.

19. You will marry while quite young and have many healthy children. Watch for an unhappy event to take place.

20. You will have someone very affectionate but with little or no financial status. Be cautious in marriage.

21. You will marry happily. This union will add to your financial means. You should enjoy life.

22. You will marry a drunk. Little success in business is evident. You will never be poor, but will be unhappy.

23. Let your conduct improve enough to command some semblance of respect. Do not neglect your lover.

24. You should have a large and virtuous family. You will have many more close friends.

25. Your travels will be prosperous if, that is, you are more prudent. Don't take unnecessary risks.

26. Many people will endeavor to bring unhappiness down upon you. You have many enemies, some who are at present posing as close and faithful friends.

27. The luck and good fortune that is ordained for you will be coveted by many others. Be more on guard.

28. Be more prudent in your conduct, since this number is very capricious. Much of your possible success will depend on your actions. This is a good number.

29. Beware, or you will be taken advantage of and deceived by the very person to whom you are devoting much attention and time. Don't rely on his or her word.

30. You love someone who is affectionate, faithful, honest, and worthy of your greatest respect and admiration.

31. You refuse too many good offers of assistance. But, be prudent when you finally do accept, or you will be more than just sorry. You may suffer financially soon.

32. You will experience very unfortunate circumstances for a short time. Be cautious and the situation will alter.

33. A fortune will soon be in your hands. Do not appear to be overanxious. Take pride in your accomplishment.

34. Alter your intentions and revise your immediate plans. You are at present on the path of ruination. Change those objectives or be prepared to suffer the consequences.

35. You will marry but will not experience true happiness. Your partner will be wealthy, but extremely jealous, suspicious, and distrustful. You may be sorry.

36. You are destined to have a sober, steady, and extremely affectionate partner. But—wealth will not be yours.

37. You are destined for sudden, unexpected prosperity. This is a number of good fortune. Expect to have a very large family.

38. The people who select this unlucky number can expect the worst unless they immediately change their mode of conduct. Justice will soon overtake you.

39. You will escape great misfortune if you remain among close friends. Do not go out on this night.

40. You will be blessed with an enormous fortune and will have no financial problems for the rest of your life. An affectionate partner, but no family, is due.

41. If, at present, you have good financial means, be charitable. If you have nothing, be frugal. Fortune is soon to smile broadly on you. Luck will change for the good.

42. You and your lover will quarrel over jealousy. Do not let this part you for long.

43. You must be willing to bear some losses with fortitude. Hold tight, for things will get better.

44. You will get a good-looking, young, and wealthy partner if you will be more patient. Don't jump into things.

45. When your conduct changes, you will surely marry a rich partner and your fortune will mend.

46. You are mixing in bad company. Disgrace will soon fall upon you. You may depend on this.

47. You are destined to have a large family. Educate your children wisely and they will honor you.

48. You are destined for misfortune at first, but don't give up too easily and success will be yours.

49. Be more on your guard and prosperity is most certainly yours. You have a number of secret enemies who are trying to do you injury.

50. Your future happiness will consist in doing good for others. No affliction can erase those pleasing spots in your memory. Do not hesitate to ask for aid.

51. You will die while still unmarried. You have been all too whimsical in the choice of a partner.

52. Your lover will soon be traveling in Europe and will be extremely successful. Be on guard against competition. You stand to lose everything.

53. You will marry, but will have little in the way of material comforts. You will receive very little affection.

54. This is always an extremely lucky number. Whatever you do will be successful. Keep plugging away.

55. After much rather serious misfortunc, you will be comfortable and happy.

56. Good conduct will produce much good luck and happiness. Do not take risks at this time.

57. Through strong feelings of affection, you will marry unhappily. But, you must make one another happy.

58. You have a multitude of lovers, but take care in choosing them or you will suffer severely for it.

59. Your lover is returning home at this time. Many severe losses have been met. Do not show your despair.

60. A letter is soon to come that will announce the loss of a great deal of money.

61. You have a secret enemy. Beware for he or she will try to do you much harm. Practice more prudence.

62. This number is a warning to be on guard against the evil consequences of idleness, either in yourself or your partner. Try to keep busy at all times.

63. Your marriage partner will be very wealthy, but also neglectful. You will suffer with boredom.

64. You will always be very poor and miserable. One child will be born and it will not be well.

65. Your sincere love from an upright heart will be amply rewarded. You are destined for a better life.

66. You will marry an older person, and are destined to be extremely unhappy. You will not want for material things.

67. A great many excellent offers will come before the one that is really worthy of your acceptance. Be cautious how this choice is ultimately made.

68. You will play the cat and mouse game until you end up losing everything. Take heed now.

69. You are being deceived by your lover. Being faithful is not one of his or her better qualities.

70. You are destined to meet with some great trouble. You must consult close friends immediately.

71. Beware! The individual you love dearly does not love you in return. He or she is seeking your downfall this very moment. Look around you and think for a moment.

72. If you jump into that marriage you will certainly be deceived. Be patient, and you will find happiness.

73. Hard work will make someone love you dearly, but it will not bring financial gain for a while.

74. You will marry and have a scolding but wealthy partner. You will not be truly happy, but you will live well.

75. You will have no children through this marriage. All kinds of wealth are yours for the asking.

76. You have a secret rival so don't let your lover deceive you with promises. Depend on this divination and you will surely better your condition.

77. You are destined to be poor financially, but rich with love and a large family.

78. Hasten your marriage. Do not delay at this point. To tarry is to lose your virtue.

79. You will have no children until later in life, but you will be addicted to intemperance.

80. Be industrious and stay honest. You will overcome that temptation and triumph over your enemies.

81. Your children will eventually make you very proud and happy, provided, that is, you see to it that they get a proper education. You will never want.

82. You are destined to fall into great difficulties. You will lose your partner and end up marrying a drunkard.

83. Your chosen mate is faithful. You will be happily married. Hasten that marriage.

84. You must immediately break off the recent friendships you have formed in haste. If you refuse, you will be poor.

85. Your lover is jealous and wishes to break up at this time. Prepare yourself for some heartache.

86. You are due to travel in Europe and Asia. You will surely marry while there. You will have a number of children, and an understanding spouse who is rich.

87. You will eventually get married, but this will take place only in advancing age. Be patient. Your mate will be a very lonely individual who is kind.

88. Beware of a secret enemy who is out to injure you in some unknown manner. Restrain the impulse to take this into your own hands. Keep your eyes open at this time.

89. You will never marry for as long as you live. You are destined to a life of being alone and unloved.

90. You will marry at least three times before settling down and being true to your mate. Each marriage will be a poor one. You stand to gain nothing.

91. The person to whom you are paying so much attention is extremely deceitful. Follow him or her after the next date.

92. If you ever do marry, you are in for a great deal of unwanted trouble. Many children will be born. Take the advice of the Golden Wheel. Remain single!

93. You will live to a ripe old age and have a life full of happiness and good times.

94. There is a young admirer dying with love for you. Take care that you are not led astray with this person. Guard against weak moments and don't spend money.

95. You will marry while in dire poverty, but will end up very wealthy if you live a quiet, serene life.

96. You are extremely whimsical and deceitful. You will not ever find true happiness with anyone.

97. At present, you have a very amorous sweetheart. Do not be flattered, for it will possibly end sooner than you might think. Do not trust this person.

98. A shocking accident will soon take place which will either involve you or your children. This will be a cause of great problems for everyone concerned.

99. You will discover that your lover is already married, or at least has no honest intention of marrying you.

100. You will have a very handsome partner in the near future. He or she will be extremely artistic, but rather unsettled. Watch for unfaithfulness.

BOOK IX
the planetary
fingers of fate

The Finger of Jupiter

If this finger is of a fair length, it shows the subject to be very
vigorous and to have a strongly instinctive nature. If this finger
is longer than the Finger of Saturn, the natural inclination will
be to rule and dominate those whom he or she comes into
contact with.

If the Finger of Jupiter is very short, it denotes a desire to
shirk or escape responsibility, and to avoid anything requiring
decisive action. If this finger is blunt, or crooked, it signifies
that the person has no sense of honor. If the Finger of Jupiter
and the Finger of Saturn are the same length, the person will
still desire to rule, but the force of personality necessary to do
this is lacking. If this finger is shorter than the Finger of Saturn,
it shows a distrustful, fearful nature. If this finger is shorter

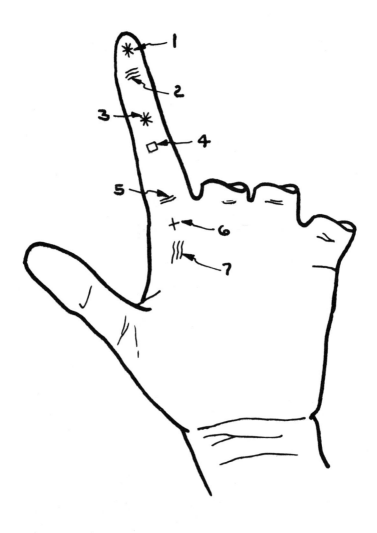

Figure 18

Signs on the Finger of Jupiter

than the Finger of Apollo, the person will be listless and completely devoid of ambition.

Lines running up the Finger of Jupiter denote an abundance of energy and a strong determination to succeed in everything attempted. If these lines are crossed, difficulties will be encountered. But if the lines continue to rise on the finger, the problems will eventually be surmounted and success will be attained.

This particular finger points towards happiness and enjoyment of the good things in life. If this finger is long in relation to the rest of the hand, the person is willing to assume great responsibility, and to take charge of important projects. The hands of those in positions of authority show marked evidence of this sign. When the finger is the same length as the one next to it, they will tend to be haughty and belligerent, because responsibility will bring on unacceptable pressures. If this finger is exceedingly long, it signifies an industrious nature combined with the ability to plan far ahead. If pointed, a brilliant mind is revealed. If this finger is square, the subject will be jolly and optimistic.

When a wide space appears between the Finger of Jupiter and the Finger of Saturn, the person will be one who thinks and decides for himself in matters of importance.

Signs found on this finger and its mount, as indicated in the accompanying illustration, indicate the following:

1. Such a star signifies a tendency towards sexual exploitation, and licentiousness. Its possessors will be completely immodest and lack virtue.

2. Three horizontal lines in this area indicate physical weakness and a tendency towards illness.

3. If there is a star here, it shows the person to be of a deceptive, mischief-making nature.

4. If there is a square in this area, it denotes that the patronage and assistance of people in high places will be readily available as needed by the subject.

5. Two lines running parallel show that a great deal of wealth will be received through an inheritance.

6. A cross appearing on the mount of Jupiter signifies fame and fortune for the individual in any field of his choice.

7. Three vertical lines here show a strong desire to do well in the business world, and to rise above the average worker.

The Finger of Saturn

If the Finger of Saturn, or the second finger, is of average length, neither long nor short, it indicates a great deal of foresight and ingenuity. If this finger is extremely long, sadness, gloom, pessimism, and depression are signified. If it is very short, the person will be seeking a life filled with pleasure, fun, and very few responsibilities.

Should this finger appear to be bent, it shows a high-strung, extremely sensitive nature. Such individuals are nervous, and they cannot take criticism even when it is offered constructively. If it is longer than the Finger of Apollo (or the Finger of the Sun), it denotes much unhappiness and a life full of problems. Such a person will not experience much success in financial matters, in love, or in other aspects of life.

When this finger is equal in length to the Finger of Apollo, the person will tend to speculate and take many risks in the money market. Gambling may well be his downfall.

Development of the joints of this finger show a desire to succeed in agricultural pursuits, and it indicates a tendency for scientific interests. If the third joint is especially long, it emphasizes this, but it also signifies a melancholy nature, and a strong desire to hoard wealth, as well as use of deceit in obtaining it.

If this finger is square-tipped, it denotes a person who is quiet, moody, and often negative and even morbid about life.

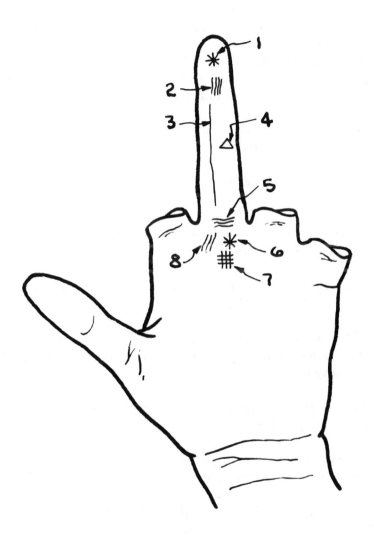

Figure 19

Signs on the Finger of Saturn

But a pointed Finger of Saturn signifies lightness of spirit, and an optimistic nature, combined with calmness and confidence.

If a number of lines go up this finger, it denotes impulsiveness, haste, and a desire to take action without thinking first. When there is a total absence of such lines, it signifies too much deliberation, and a lack of initiative.

Signs found on this finger and its mount, as indicated on the accompanying illustration, indicate the following:

1. A star in this location means great sorrow or trouble to be caused by a lack of prudence.

2. Several vertical lines show that the person's desire to gain wealth is too great, and that this should be curbed.

3. Long vertical lines indicate sadness and morbidness. An individual with such lines may consider suicide.

4. A triangle located in this area denotes a great deal of misfortune, trouble, and possible failure, with financial losses.

5. Three parallel lines in this area of the finger, either vertical or horizontal, predict good fortune and great success in all competitive things.

6. Such a star on the base of this finger signifies murder or death by some violent agency.

7. A grille in this location predicts sorrow of great magnitude, insurmountable problems, and serious trouble close at hand.

8. Vertical lines in this area of the finger denote the death of a relative or a very close friend. Each line signifies one death.

The Finger of Apollo (or the Sun)

This finger refers to wealth and art. If it is pointed, the artistic tendencies in the individual will predominate. If it is shaped like a spatula, the person will be even more actively engaged in artistic pursuits. Such people often become great actors or actresses, and are noted for their eloquence. A square-ended Finger of Apollo signifies reasoning power and good logic.

If the Finger of Apollo is shorter than the Finger of Jupiter, the individual will be destined to rule in matters regarding both business and family life. The subject's ambition and desire will overrule his common sense and reasoning power. If it is nearly the same length as the Finger of Apollo, it denotes great ambition, and a strong desire for wealth and fame. If both of these fingers are the same length, the individual will excel in the pursuit of all artistic and intellectual endeavors. If the Finger of Apollo is longer than the Finger of Jupiter, it is a mark of certain success in any undertaking. If this finger is much longer than the Finger of Jupiter, the person will covet wealth, honor, glory and fame above all else in his life.

If the Finger of Apollo is a little shorter than the Finger of Saturn, a desire to take unnecessary risks will be felt, but this practice can be rigidly controlled. Such an individual will be extremely talented and have a great love for artistic things. If these two fingers are equal in length, it signifies a desire for financial speculation and a love of gambling in all forms. Great risks will be taken by such people. If the Finger of Apollo is much longer than the Finger of Saturn, it denotes an even greater desire to gamble in the game of life. Such a person is inclined to be rather reckless, and may endanger his life through this. If this finger tends to be unusually short, the individual is not a lover of art and beauty, and in fact will be quite indifferent to it. If the finger is bent, the artistic tendencies are being channeled in the wrong direction. Such a person may become involved in pornographic endeavors.

If the Finger of Apollo is equal in length to the Finger of Mercury, the individual will be extremely changeable. He will be amiable one moment and argumentative the next. The remaining conditions in the hand will show whether or not this will be used in a positive manner to benefit the person possessing it. If this finger is much longer than the Finger of

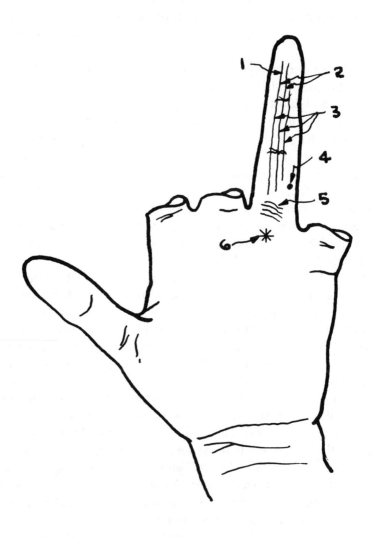

Figure 20

Signs on the Finger of Apollo

Mercury, it signifies that the desire to do well artistically will overcome all business ambition, and that success will be forthcoming.

Signs found on this finger and its mount, as indicated on the accompanying illustration, indicate the following:

1. A long vertical line shows good fortune and fame.

2. Two vertical lines signify great honor and wealth.

3. Three or more vertical lines denote financial losses caused by members of the opposite sex. It also represents a deep understanding and love for artistic things. If these lines are cut deeply, and very clear, some type of art will be pursued with great enthusiasm.

4. A spot in any area of the finger signifies the danger of a serious scandal concerning the individual who possesses it.

5. Cross lines such as shown here are always signs of some misfortune and unhappiness in the person's life.

6. If a star occurs on the mount of this finger, the person will acquire wealth through speculation and chance, but not from hard work and honest labor. If a number of lines accompany this star, it emphasizes the fact that wealth will be accumulated. If these lines are indistinct, it indicates that the person will not marry, but if they do, it will be for financial gain rather than for love.

The Finger of Mercury

If the Finger of Mercury is well shaped and long, it is like the upper joint of the thumb in denoting strong willpower, and a talent for influencing others to the person's way of thinking. It shows a nature dedicated to self-improvement. If this finger is unduly long, and almost reaches the nail of the next finger, it signifies a fluency of the tongue and the pen. If the little finger comes above the top joint of the third finger, the person will be domineering, harsh and, difficult to befriend. He must always have things his way, or not at all, and feel extreme pangs of jealousy. If this finger does not quite reach the top joint of the next finger, such a person will be obedient, kind, and very easy to dominate. He will be happy to let his spouse run things around the house.

The examination of the hands of many married couples will show that, in the case of a great number of happy marriages, the little finger of one mate will reach above the joint of the third finger, while this will not be so in the case of the other partner.

If this finger is too long, it signifies a scheming, crafty, unpleasant disposition. If it is too short, the person will tend to form hasty conclusions and will lack a sense of judgment. If it equals the length of the Finger of Apollo, leadership is revealed, but so is some dishonesty and cheating.

If this finger is equal or nearly so with the Finger of Jupiter, it shows a diplomatic nature, and a politically oriented mind. This may lead to a position of authority. Such an individual will be able to make friends with others who are in power at the moment, whether he likes them or not. If this finger is nearly as long as the Finger of Saturn, it indicates an interest in, and a natural inclination for, scientific subjects.

If the Finger of Mercury has a large nail joint, this too indicates a fondness for writing or other artistic endeavors. The person will be extremely industrious, but may be somewhat dishonest. If this finger is bent, dishonesty is further indicated. A wide space between the Finger of Mercury and the Finger of Apollo, is a sign that the person will be independent in thought, speech and action. If the Finger of Mercury is pointed, the individual will be eloquent, and will have an aptitude for winning arguments by capitalizing on his strong intuitive nature. A square-tipped Finger of Mercury shows good judgment and reasoning ability. An active mind is noted, as well as an ability to explain and illustrate things clearly. This would be desirable for many professions.

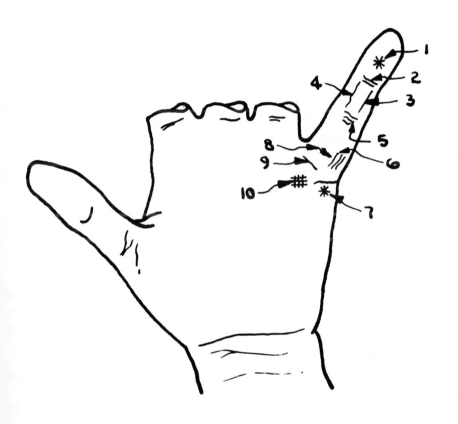

Figure 21

Signs on the Finger of Mercury

Signs found on this finger and its mount, as indicated on the accompanying illustration, indicate the following:

1. A star in this area, or on the joint itself, indicates a single life. The person will never marry, and will not do well in other areas of life.

2. Deep and heavy lines in the joint show a lack of muscular coordination, and physical weakness.

3. A line passing from the second to the third joint, is a sign of oratorical powers which will bring good fortune.

4. A wavy line extending from the second to the third joint, is an indication of a sharp mind and a scheming nature.

5. A series of weak, wavering lines appearing in this joint signify a weakness of spirit and a lack of initiative.

6. Three or more vertical lines at the base of this finger show that the person is addicted to fads, theories, and impractical dreams and goals in life.

7. If a star appears in this area, expect dishonesty from the person who possesses it.

8. If such lines appear to be indistinct and crossed, it denotes a coarse or gross person.

9. One horizontal line shows excellence of character. Good fortune will surely attend such an individual.

10. A grille appearing in this area denotes a tendency to steal, and the ability to tell lies with a straight face. Never put trust in such a person for he will eventually take advantage of anyone who does.

Signs on the Fingernails

If the nail on the Finger of Saturn shows a white mark, it denotes a long journey to be taken in the near future. If this mark appears to be black instead, it signifies an impending disaster of great consequence.

If the nail on the Finger of Mercury has a white spot, it is a sign of successful business enterprises. A black spot portends great financial losses and business disaster. Any other nail having black marks on it is an indication of sorrow and trouble.

If a white star-shaped mark appears on any nail, it is a sign that the person deeply loves someone, but that this affection is not being returned. If it appears on the thumb, it indicates that the affection will be returned.

Any nails that are wide and long show a disposition inclined to gentleness and kindness, and one who is uncertain and inconsistent. Such individuals are subject to many diseases, and will be under the influence of the opposite sex at all times. They are generally rather fleshy, jolly but moody, and undependable. If a white mark appears at the extremity of the nail, it reveals much misfortune in financial affairs.

Nails that are of medium length and width, and of a bluish tint, indicate extreme nervousness and bad blood circulation. If the root of any nail shows a red color of mixed shading, it signifies a combative nature. If the apex of the nail is darkly shaded or black, the ambitions and goals of the person are not very high. Nails that are red and spotted indicate a warlike nature, and an individual who is cruel and spiteful. The number of red spots will reveal the number of evil desires the person has. Such individuals cannot be trusted in any situation. Nails that are pale show a sickly nature, and one who is subject to many diseases.

Nails that are slender and narrow show a nature inclined to domineer others. Such people prey on the weaknesses of those who are less intelligent or powerful. They will not be able to get along with anyone, even relatives or friends. They will be, as

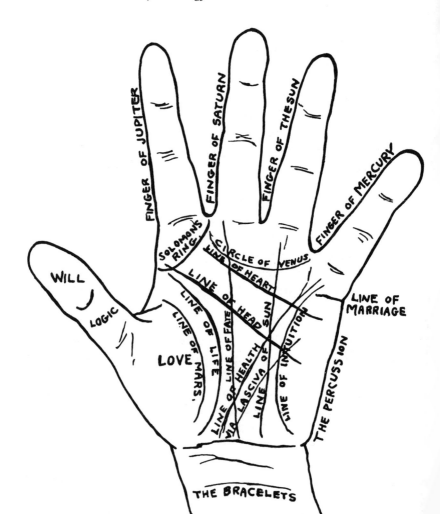

Figure 22

A map of the hand that clearly designates the planetary fingers as they have been accepted for centuries by all astrologists. This illustration appeared in Revelations of the Hand, by Dr. Alex J. McIvor-Tyndall prior to 1900.

one ancient astrologer expresses it, "like an eagle commanding lesser birds, killing them, or displaying power of lofty flight to others less fortunate."

Nails that are short denote people who are athletic and very intuitive. They are destined to marry while quite young, and are anxious matchmakers for others. Nails that are square and short indicate a tendency towards heart ailments. If the nails on a woman's hand are found to be short, and if her fingers possess knots, be assured that she will rule her husband, and that he will submit to her fancies if domestic peace is desired. Small, crooked nails, or nails bent at the apex, show a proud, ambitious, and very courageous nature.

Nails that are thick, bent, and long, show a cruel nature, and the person who is greedy and lustful. Nails that are long, curved, thin, and ribbed, show a tendency towards mental illness and bronchial trouble.

Nails that are long and slender show a person to be very friendly and agreeable, but one who does not confide in others. These individuals have learned to be deceitful, and to use this capability to further themselves. Oblique nails further emphasize this trait of deceit. Such persons will delight in getting the best of a friend. They will lack courage, be dishonest in their dealings, and will be extremely vain regarding themselves.

BOOK X
mystic influences
of precious stones

The legendary history of precious stones is certainly a study in itself, and a number of ancient treatises have been seriously written on this subject. This is not meant to be a complete anthology, but instead represents a cross-section of the old expositions written by those who firmly believed in the occult virtues possessed by such stones.

Signification of Gems and Stones
in a Girdle:

Agate—*Safety through all*
Basalt—*Stability*
Cacholong—*Truth, fidelity*
Crocidolite—*Fidelity*
Diaspore—*A warning*

Egyptian pebble—*Intellect*
Firestone—*Excitement*
Granite—*Eternal life*
Heliotrope—*Great wisdom*
Iolite—*Security*

Jasper—*Great courage*
Lapis lazuli—*Love of luxury*
Malachite—*Joyfulness*
Nephrite—*Good health*
Onyx—*Conjugal felicity*
Porphyry—*Great endurance*
Quartz agate—*Security*
Rose quartz—*Great fortune*

Sardonyx—*Willingness to love*
Turquoise—*Cheer and joy*
Ultramarine—*Artistic*
Verd antique—*Worthiness*
Wood opal—*Simplicity*
Xylotile—*New discoveries*
Yellow crystal—*Fate*
Zurlite—*Aloofness*

In a Diadem:

Amethyst—*Protection*
Beryl—*Blissfulness*
Chrysoberyl—*Benevolence*
Cyanite—*Honesty*
Diamond—*Repentance*
Emerald—*Conquest*
Feldspar—*Punctuality*
Garnet—*Companionship*
Hyacinth—*Rest and sleep*
Idocrase—*Consistency, firmness*
Jacinth—*Unpretentiousness*
Lynx sapphire—*Prophetic*
Milk opal—*Chastity*

Natrolite—*Optimism and hope*
Opal—*Innocence and purity*
Pyrope—*Kindness*
Quartz—*Guardianship*
Ruby—*Charitableness*
Sapphire—*Great faith*
Topaz—*Faithfulness*
Uranite—*Great hopes*
Water sapphire—*Good fortune*
Xanthoconite—*Stability
of mind*
Yellow tourmaline—*Strength*
Zircon—*Visionary*

In a Bridal Ring:

The ring itself symbolizes a pure and unending relationship.

Asbestos—*Unrelenting love*
Agate—*Health, long life*
Beryl—*Mutual love*
Carnelian—*Patience*
Diamond—*Virtue*

Emerald—*Marital stability*
Lodestone—*Persuasion*
Opal—*Hopefulness*
Pearl—*Purity, chastity*
Sapphire—*Faith*

Birthday Gems and Stones:

January—The Garnet: *a symbol of stability and firmness.*
February—The Amethyst: *a symbol of sincerity.*
March—The Bloodstone: *a symbol of great courage.*
April—The Diamond: *a symbol of innocence and chastity.*
May—The Emerald: *a symbol of success in love matters.*
June—The Agate: *a symbol of health and a long life.*
July—The Carnelian and the Ruby: *symbols of contentment.*
August—The Sardonyx: *a symbol of matrimonial bliss.*
September—The Sapphire: *a symbol of strength.*
October—The Opal: *a symbol of good luck and optimism.*
November—The Topaz: *a symbol of love, friendship and fidelity.*
December—The Turquoise: *a symbol of prosperity.*

The Sentiments Expressed by Gems and Precious Stones:

The following table has been prepared with great care and should always be consulted when sending or receiving gifts of precious stones. The hidden meanings of each stone is interpreted as given below.

absence: *fluorite*
adversity cannot defeat you: *fire opal*
affability: *cat sapphire*
amiability: *vermeil*
approval of you: *moss opal*

be not vain: *clouded marble*
brilliant successes: *ruby*

changeable disposition: *hornstone*
charitable: *chrysoberyl*
　　　　ruby
childlike purity: *rock crystal*
close attachment: *Bohemian diamond*
courage and strength: *bloodstone*

danger and evil premonitions: *cat's-eye*
despair and depression: *striped jasper*
dignified feelings: *ruby*
disappointment: *chrysolite*
disdain and scorn: *amber*
divine strength and power: *ruby*
domestic bliss: *Balas ruby*

faith and hope: *sapphire*
faithfulness in friendship: *emerald*
amethyst
lava
topaz
felicity in love: *garnet*
fidelity in love and matrimony: *Bohemian topaz*
firmness and strong will: *Rock of Gibralter stone*
first feelings of love: *satin gypsum*
friendship is desired: *emerald*
sunstone
friendship is offered: *carnelian*
friendship, woman's: *natrolite*

generosity: *tourmaline*
freestone
good works: *sapphire*
great beauty: *serpentine*
great fortune: *rose quartz*

happy love: *emerald*
hard-hearted and cold: *flint*
health and happiness: *agate*
hope and optimism: *aquamarine*
humility and lack of pride: *opal*
jasper
pearl
white marble

I am innocent: *pearls*
I am living in the past: *lepidolite*
I feel an innocent love: *red granite*
I will not cease loving you: *satin spar*

joyfulness: *diamond*
justice and fairness: *idocrase*

leadership: *carnelian*
life, happy: *diamond*
life, long: *agate*
love: *ruby*
love of the arts: *lapis lazuli*
love's ambition: *cachelong*

marital love and devotion: *onyx*
marriage, poor: *hyalite*
married happiness: *sardoin*
mental beauty: *corundum*
mirthfulness: *Egyptian pebble*
modesty and purity: *opal*
mourning and sadness: *jet*
mysterious thoughts: *atinite*

noble character: *lapis lazuli*

patience: *chrysoberyl*
peace of mind: *carnelian*
pride: *diamond*
prosperity and wealth: *onyx*
purity and loveliness: *jasper*
pure and chaste: *alabaster*

remember me always: *jade*
                    rose quartz
resigned to my fate: *Egyptian jasper*
respect for you: *zircon*
riches: *occidental turquoise*

sad tidings and feelings: *agate*
safety in all things: *coral*
self-love: *prase*
silent expressions of love: *chlorophane*
sincerity in all things: *amethyst*
stability and firmness: *amazonstone*
                                       spinelle
success and good fortune: *turquoise*
sun of my whole being: *hypersthane*
suspicious of you: *bottle stone*

thoughtful contemplation: *sapphire*
thoughtful friendship: *moonstone*
true friendship: *garnet*
truth in everything: *rainbow agate*

unchanging friendship: *natrolite*
unfortunate love: *jade*

victory over all obstacles: *beryl*

warning of great dangers: *moonstone*
welcome: *apyrite*
whimsical love: *labradorite*
wisdom in your thoughts: *bloodstone*

you are a phony: *nephritis*

Stones for Lovers:

The following ten verses of poetry were taken from *The Lapidarium of Marbodus,* an eleventh-century Latin poetry manuscript.

Diamond
Hardness invincible which naught can tame,
Untouched by steel, unconquered by flame.

Beryl
This potent gem, found in far India's mines,
With mutual love the wedded couple binds.

Asbestos
Kindled once, it no extinction knows;
But with eternal fire, unceasing glows.

Agate
The agate on the wearer strength bestows;
With ruddy health his fresh complexion glows;
Both eloquence and grace by it are given.
He gains the favor both of earth and heaven.

Pearl
Prized as an ornament, its whiteness gleams,
And well the robe and well the gold beseems.

Loadstone
The Loadstone peace to wrangling couples grants,
And mutual love in wedded hearts implants;
It gives the power to argue and teach,
Grace to the tongue, persuasion to the speech.

Opal
This stone for color might an emerald seem;
But drops of blood diversify the green;
It gifts the wearer with prophetic eye
Into the future's darkest depths to spy.

Carnelian
Fate has with virtues great its nature graced;
Tied round the neck, or on the finger placed.
Its friendly influence checks the rising fray,
And chases spite and quarrels far away.

Emerald
Of all green things which bounteous earth supplies,
Nothing in greenness with the emerald vies;
Unchanged by sun or shade, its lustre glows;
The blazing lamp on it no dimness throws.

Sapphire
As gem of gems, above all others placed,
By nature with superior honors graced;
E'en Heaven is moved by its force divine
To list to vows presented at its shrine.

Stones for Birthdays:

The following twelve verses of poetry were taken from an old set of character pamphlets last published in 1910. They cover every month of the year.

By those who in January are born
No gem save GARNET should be worn;
They will insure you constancy,
True friendship and fidelity.

The February-born will find
Sincerity and peace of mind,
Freedom from passion and from care,
If they the AMETHYST will wear.

Who in this world of ours their eyes
In March first open shall be wise,
In days of peril firm and brave,
And wear a BLOODSTONE to their grave.

Those who in April date their years
DIAMONDS should wear, lest bitter tears
For vain repentance flow. This stone
Emblem of innocence is known.

Who first beholds the light of day
In Spring's sweet flowery month of May,
And wears the EMERALD all her life,
Shall be a loved and happy wife.

Who comes with summer to this earth
And owes to June her day of birth,
With ring of AGATE upon her hand,
Can health, wealth and peace command.

The glowing RUBY should adorn
Those who in warm July are born;
Thus will she be exempt and free
From love's doubts and anxiety.

Wear a SARDONYX, or for thee
No conjugal felicity;
The August-born, without this stone,
'Tis said, must live unloved alone.

A maiden born when Autumn's leaves
Are rustling in September's breeze
A SAPPHIRE on her brow should bind;
Twill cure diseases of the mind.

October's child is born for woe,
And life's vicissitudes must know;
But lay an OPAL on her breast,
And hope will lull those woes to rest.

Who first comes to this world below
With dear November's fog and snow
Should prize the TOPAZ's amber hue,
Emblem of friends and lovers true.

If cold December gave you birth,
The month of snow and ice and mirth,
Place on your head a TURQUOISE blue;
Success will bless you if you do.

BOOK XI
the twelve houses
and their power

Each of the twelve houses is a distinct and independent figure involving a separate problem of fate. If a person desires only to know a single phase of his destiny, it will be necessary only to erect the house that governs the type of events required to be foreseen. But this can only give a partial and generally unsatisfactory glimpse of the future. Astrology is a candid, as well as a profound science. It aims not only at the truth, but the whole truth. The fortune indicated by one of the celestial houses may possibly be modified by the planetary influences of the others. Therefore, a full nativity, one covering the entire celestial circle, should be calculated.

It must not ever be assumed that the nativity of an individual must always take place simply because the horoscope indicates certain events. A disastrous nativity is *not* bound by the whim of some supernatural or universal power. Much of the responsibility rests with the person himself. If a certain date portends some terrible misfortune in a specific circumstance, the disaster can often be avoided if the person does not place himself in such a situation as to encounter the difficulty.

The first thing to be ascertained prior to the construction of a horoscope, or map of life, is the hour of conception *and* the hour of birth. Perhaps the best means of arriving at these important facts is by the *Method of Hermes.* Having obtained the estimated time of birth, the astrologer erects his figure, and proceeds to calculate the position of the Moon in relation thereto. He then takes the distance of the Moon from the horoscope and after completing a number of other important calculations, he enters his figures in the table of the child's house. The precise number of days between the conception and the birth will appear against the signs and degrees he has calculated. He then proceeds to inquire as to which planets ruled at the time of birth, and to erect his twelve celestial houses, corresponding in number to the signs of the zodiac.

As illustrations for the guidance of astrological students, horoscopes of three individuals who have played important, though very dissimilar parts on the world's stage—Marcus Tullius Cicero, Oliver Cromwell, and Henry VIII—are reproduced from the most authentic records available. Each horoscope was cast by William Lilly, the most eminent astrologer of the seventeenth century.

The following are brief outlines of the order, nature, and predominating influences of the twelve celestial or zodiacal houses or compartments. They constitute, as a whole, a complete horoscope, and they vary in their indications according to the planets found in them at the time of the native's birth, and of course, the position and power of such planets.

The Twelve Houses

The First House: This is the house of life and refers to the life of an individual; his stature and shape, the qualities of his mind, his complexion, etc. It is called the angle of the east, the horoscope ascendant or horizon, because when the Sun or any planet touches its cusp or point, it begins to rise and appear visible in our hemisphere. Much depends upon the aspects and conjunctions of the planets found in this house—the morals, the manners, the passions, and, to some extent, the fortune of the native depend upon its ruling influences. The stars and planets placed within this house exert a most powerful effect on the future life and destiny of the individual whose horoscope it constitutes. Saturn or Mars within this house, never fail to denote sickness or accidents. Jupiter and Venus in a similar

Figure 23

The Horoscope of Marcus Tullius Cicero

position, insure freedom, good fortune, and lasting success. This house is of the masculine gender and rules the head and face as the sign *Aries.*

The Second House: The second house in order from the ascendants relates especially to the estate and fortune of the native. It is commonly called "the house of riches." It was named Anaphora by the Greeks. This house signifies the pecuniary success of the individual for whom the horoscope was cast. It includes such things as houses, lands, gold, gain or loss in business, poverty, misfortune, and everything bearing any relationship to wealth. The financial success of the native depends upon the ascendant planet in this house at the time of birth. It is a highly important celestial compartment, and it should be studied with thoughtfulness and calculated with care by the astrologer. It is represented by the sign *Taurus.*

The Third House: This house is that of family connections, relatives, friends, letters, messages, rumors, journeys, etc. Although this house doesn't affect the personal interests of the native as much as does the second house, it bears strongly on friendships, love of family, and social ties, in general. The early astrologers utilized this house to form all judgments respecting the good or evil fate of both friends and relatives of the native. When the evil or unfortunate stars were found to be located in this part of the zodiac, evil effects were necessarily said to follow. For example, when Saturn appears, hatred is found to exist among members of the family. If Uranus appears in this house, the native will never be able to settle down in one place, and he will not be very close to his family. Mars situated in this house is a sign of great evil. This house is represented by the sign *Gemini.*

The Fourth House: The lower angle of heaven, whose line the Sun touches at midnight, is more feeble in influence than any other angle throughout the celestial circle, and is termed the fourth house. This house exerts special influence upon all questions affecting the private enemies of children, and upon those regarding secret plots against children. It also has a bearing upon the lands, houses, inheritances, and the dwelling of the native. It represents the father and his quality and condition. The Roman soothsayers termed it *Imum Caeli,* or "bottom of heaven." It signifies the conclusion or end of everything and, according to the planet—whether favorable or malign—which rules this house at birth, the native may be wealthy, distinguished, and successful, or he may be a murderer, a thief, or even an adulterer. This house is represented by the sign *Cancer.*

The Fifth House: This house denotes the condition, qualities, and fortunes of the native's children. It also represents his

Figure 24

The Horoscope of Oliver Cromwell

pleasures—such as plays, banquets, parties, revelings, etc. The Greek astrologers called it "joy," or "delight," from the happiness parents are supposed to derive from their offspring, or expect to receive from them. Malign planets posted in this house may portend the death of the native's children or, should they survive, their disobedience. If, on the other hand, the house is governed by favorable planets, the native will derive infinite comfort and consolation from his offspring. Unfortunate or unfavorable planets may also signify great losses to the native in the prosecution of his pleasures. This house also points to the death of monarchs and world leaders, and to the journeys of religious persons. It is a masculine house which rules the liver, heart, sides, back, and stomach, and is represented by the sign *Leo*.

The Sixth House: This house is generally evil, for it portends sickness, disease, and secret enemies. It indicates the curability and incurability of diseases according to the ruling influences. It also denotes the medicines most appropriate for the amelioration of pain and the regaining of health. The nature of the ailment as well as its intensity is indicated by the position of the stellar orbs in relation to this important house. Too much thought, study, and research cannot be bestowed on this division of the celestial circle. It is a feminine house represented by the sign *Virgo*.

The Seventh House: This house affects marriage and conjugal happiness. It portrays the character of the person to whom the native is to be united in wedlock. It also represents his enemies, lawsuits, arguments, etc. This house is entitled to much serious consideration because happiness in life so often depends on marriage. When uncongenial planets are in the ascendent, the probabilities are in favor of unhappy unions and unfortunate disputes. On the other hand, the predominance of planets deemed to be fortunate exercise a happy influence in this house, for they portend a felicitous wedded life and prosperity. If the evil planets Saturn or Mars occupy this house, and their powerful influence is not counteracted by the mild beams of Venus, the native will, assuredly, be unfortunate in marriage as well as in continual turmoil in other areas of his life. This house is the oracle of love, wars, and a describer of thieves; it is a masculine constellation represented by the sign *Libra.*

The Eighth House: This house is important because it is said to answer all questions in relation to wills, legacies, adversaries, friends, and success in life. If Jupiter or Venus are in this constellation, the native cannot die a violent death. This house relates to the death of the native and all things connected with

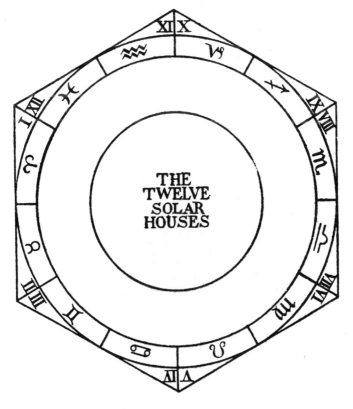

Figure 25

The Twelve Solar Houses

death. All astrologers, from the time of the Phoenicians to the present day, have deemed this house to be malignant, unfortunate, and portentous of evil, unless strong counteracting influences should neutralize its primary signification. There is no part in the division of the zodiac so absolutely malign and cruel as is this house. It is a feminine house represented by the sign *Scorpio.*

The Ninth House: This house is called *metus a mutur,* from fear or doubt. Astrologers call it the house of religion, because even the most pious persons frequently doubt the sufficiency of

Figure 26

The Horoscope of Henry VIII

their faith, and fear that they shall never attain the degree of purity conceived to be necessary for their everlasting welfare. It represents the dreams and visions of the native, his scientific knowledge, his voyages or journeys, and ecclesiastical honors. It answers all questions concerning religion, science, learning, books, and travels. Whether the native will be skeptical, unbelieving, superstitious, or zealous in religious matters depends on the planets located in this house at the time of birth. The prosperity or disaster attached to journeys is also dependent on the same thing. This house, under certain planetary conjunctions, may render the native skillful in interpreting visions and dreams. It is a masculine house represented by *Sagittarius.*

The Tenth House: This house was called *cor caeli* by the Latin astrologers, and *medium caeli*—the heart or the middle of heaven. It is the house of dignity, honor, authority, and preferment of the native. It also refers to the native's mother, regarding her rank in society. Although deemed to be generally favorable, this house can be unfortunate if certain planets are found in it at birth. Jupiter, Venus, or the Sun denote great eminence in life, and the Moon portends honors and high position. Gloomy and malignant Saturn foretells of disgrace and ruin if it isn't opposed by other more benevolent stars. The Duke of Wellington was born under the benign influence of Jupiter in this house, while Napoleon was born under the evil influence of Saturn in the same. Is not this a splendid illustration of the accuracy of astrological predictions? It is a feminine house represented by the sign *Capricorn.*

The Eleventh House: There is a remarkable unanimity of opinion between ancient and modern astrologers in relation to the important astrological influences of this house. It was known among the Romans as *bonus genius*—the "good demon, angel, or spirit." All questions are answered from this house concerning friends, desires, wishes, hopes, flatterers, and favorites. It confers favor, a good disposition, and fulfillment of the native's expectations. If this house is infested with evil planets, the native will experience severe disappointment. Saturn is ominous of evil and signifies disappointment of all joyful anticipations, and a great deal of discord and sorrow in families and among friends. The Sun in this house denotes many friends of all ages who will give important assistance to the native. The Moon exerts a favorable sway over the destiny of the native. This house is masculine and represented by the sign *Aquarius*.

The Twelfth House: This house indicates the imprisonments, sufferings, banishments, and private enemies of the native. It also refers to horses and farm stock if he happens to possess any. In horary astrology it would signify sorrow, unceasing persecution, murder, assassination, and envy. The Latins called

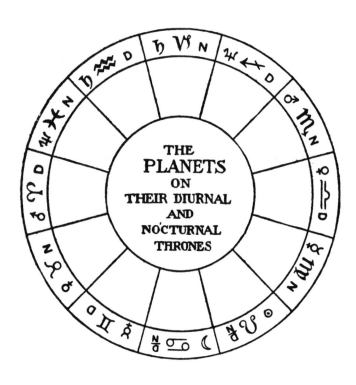

Figure 27

The Planets

this house *malus genius,* the "evil angel," or the "evil spirit." It is a fearfully unfortunate house. If Saturn is found in it at birth, fear, sorrow, exile, captivity, and all sorts of trouble are forecast. Jupiter, found in this house, indicates reproach, persecution, and poverty. Mars denotes imprisonment through errors and willful crimes. This house is feminine and represented by the sign *Pisces.*

BOOK XII
astrological
anatomy

A person born when the first part of the sign *Aries* is rising will have a small raised mole among the hairs of the head. If the second part of this sign happened to be rising at birth, the mark or mole would then be seen on the forehead, and it would be raised in the form of a pea or a wart. If the third part of Aries arose at birth, the mark would appear below the mouth, or toward the chin. Those persons having these marks on any part of the body described, will also generally have the mark of Mars in the lowest part of the body, this too in the form of a raised mole or wart.

An ancient Italian astrologer says that "women with brown, hairy moles on the chin, especially if these excrescences are on the under part of the chin, are industrious, active, and are good housewives." They are also, he states, "very sanguine and given to love follies. They talk much and whilst they are easily excited to return a love which is offered them, they are not so readily prevailed upon to become indifferent." He then goes on to say that "For this reason, they should be treated with circumspect, calm friendship and kept at a distance by a mildly cold dignity of demeanour." In passing on to another remark concerning moles, he states that a "mole upon the upper lip, especially if it is bristly, will be found in no person who is not defective in something essential." He does not mention whether this deficiency is of a moral, mental, or a physical nature.

The general physical description of those born under the influence of Aries is as follows: They are not very tall, but are above middle stature, rather lean or spare, but physically strong with large bones, and possessing a long scraggy neck and thick shoulders. The facial features will be long, and the eyes particularly brilliant and piercing. The eyebrows are bushy and black, while the hair is sandy or even carroty, and the complexion sallow, dusky, or swarthy.

The common ailments are generally those of the feverish, eruptive types. This would encompass such things as smallpox, measles, ringworm, pimples or boils, paralysis, toothache, swellings, headaches, baldness, and other things directly affecting the nervous system, or the brain itself.

When *Taurus* is rising at birth, the native of this sign bears a mark on the front of the throat, sometimes shaped like a strawberry or a reddish-tinted mole. Such a mark always has ill effects on the person. Should the second part of the Taurus sign be rising at the nativity, the person will have the same type of mark at the side of the throat. If the third part of the sign is rising at birth, the same mark appears at the nape of the neck, in which case it will be more raised than the initial two mentioned.

Persons born within the rule of Taurus, if no counteracting planetary influences exist, are usually remarkably stout and athletic. They are strong and well coordinated, but rather dull and apathetic. The forehead is broad, as are the shoulders, and the hands are extremely gross. Such individuals have a short neck, a large face and eyes, thick lips, and curly, very coarse, dark hair.

Index Chart.

Parts of the Grand Man Relating to the	Signs.	Domain of the Signs.	Date of the Signs.
	♈ Aries.	Fire.	Mch. 21 to Apr. 19.
	♉ Taurus.	Earth.	Apr. 19 to May 20.
	♊ Gemini.	Air.	May 20 to June 21
	♋ Cancer.	Water.	June 21 to July 22.
	♌ Leo.	Fire.	July 22 to Aug. 22
	♍ Virgo.	Earth.	Aug. 22 to Sept. 23
	♎ Libra.	Air.	Sept. 23 to Oct. 23.
	♏ Scorpio.	Water.	Oct. 23 to Nov. 22.
	♐ Sagittarius.	Fire.	Nov. 22 to Dec. 21
	♑ Capricorn.	Earth.	Dec. 21 to Jan. 20.
	♒ Aquarius.	Air.	Jan. 20 to Feb. 19.
	♓ Pisces.	Water.	Feb. 19 to Mch. 21.

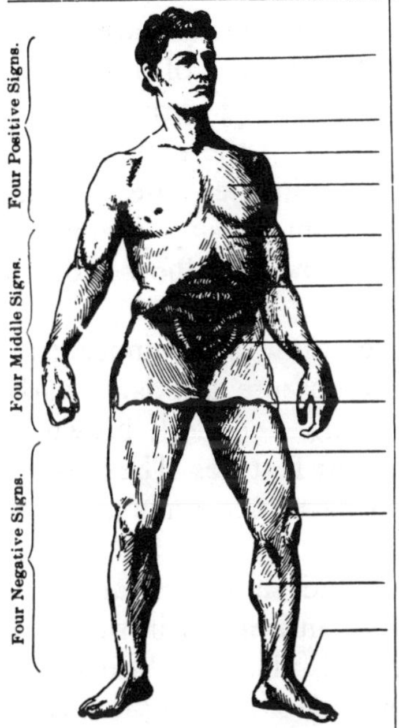

Four Positive Signs. — Four Middle Signs. — Four Negative Signs.

The Four Triplicities.

Domains.	Head.	Middle.	Negative.
Fire..................	Aries.	Leo.	Sagittarius.
Earth.......	Taurus.	Virgo.	Capricorn.
Air..................	Gemini.	Libra.	Aquarius.
Water..............	Cancer.	Scorpio.	Pisces.

Figure 28

The anatomy of a man's body is said to be carefully governed by the various signs of the zodiac. This excellent illustration seems to have appeared first in a privately printed book Wonders of Astrology, *1833, and, subsequently, in* Influence of the Zodiac, *1894.*

The diseases and other illnesses attached to Taurus people are such things as depression, consumption, tuberculosis of ·the lymphatic glands, inflammation of the respiratory passages, sore throats, skin tumors around the scalp area, and abscesses around the neck and throat areas which are governed by this sign.

Those born under the influence of *Gemini* have their marks on their arms and shoulders. If the first part of this sign arose at birth, the mark will be borne on the right arm. If the second part of this sign is rising at the time of the nativity, a mole or wart will appear on the left arm, in the same area near the shoulder. If the third part of the sign is rising, the native bears the mark on the right arm, but below the elbow and generally close to the wrist.

The influence of Gemini gives those born under it a ruddy complexion, not clear, but more obscure and dark. Dark hazel eyes which are quick and piercing, and dark brown, almost black hair are two other prominent features. They are tall and erect, in constant motion, and have long arms and legs with fleshy hands and feet.

This sign controls the arms and shoulders, and therefore denotes all diseases, accidents, or infirmities in these areas, as well as some other more general illnesses: headaches, liver ailments, fits of insanity, and anemia are a few; it also signifies fractures, bruises and cuts around the arms and shoulders, as well as falls from high places, and a multitude of nervous disorders.

When the sign of *Cancer* is in the ascendant, a mark will appear on the upper right breast in the shape of a flower. Such a wart or mole will be of a whitish color, and will commonly be seen to have a hair or two sprouting from it. In days gone by, this mark was always thought to be evidence of a woman being a witch, and those having it were immediately put to death. Those born under the second part of the Cancer sign rising have a wart or mole lower down on the right breast, while those whose birth takes place while the third part of this sign is rising will find one under the breast.

This constellation is the house of the Moon and exaltation of Jupiter. It produces a fair or pale complexion, one which often seems rather sickly. The facial features are generally round, the eyes a mild blue, the voice very weak, the hair a sad brown, and the overall stature is small, with the upper parts of the body larger than the lower.

The breast and stomach areas are governed by Cancer, and the various ailments are many. These cover such things as cancer, especially of the breast, asthma, coughs, shortness of breath, pleurisy, dropsy, consumption, and a loss of appetite. If evil stars are angular to this sign, there is a great danger of eventual insanity.

When *Leo* is in the ascendant at birth, the wart or mole will appear on the left breast, and in the same manner, if the mark appears high up on the breast, it signifies that the first part of Leo was ascending. A person born when the second part of the sign is rising will find the mark on the middle of the left breast. If the mole or wart appears on one side, usually towards the left armpit, the third part of Leo must have been ascending at birth.

Such people have large bodies, broad shoulders, muscular builds, and curling blond or dark flaxen hair. They appear to be very stern, have full and round eyes, a ruddy complexion, an oval face, and an unmusical voice, yet one that is powerful. If the last portion of Leo is in ascension, it produces a correspondingly weaker body with fairer hair, and an effeminate nature.

Since this sign governs the heart and back, its diseases and other ailments will be centered in these areas. Fainting, fevers, convulsions, and inflammations, in general, are included. All afflictions in the sides and ribs will be prevalent. Pains in the back, pleurisy, heart tremors, and jaundice may strike without warning. Other illnesses could possibly be such things as sore eyes, smallpox, and measles.

In nativities governed by *Virgo,* the mole or wart will be found on the upper part of the stomach, between the under part of the two breasts, when the first part of the sign is in ascendancy. Those born while the second part of the sign is rising will have a mark near the navel, while those born under the influence of the third part of a rising Virgo will be marked quite low down on the belly area. Such people who are so marked are extremely inconsistent. Every mole or wart created by the power of Virgo will be flat and reddish in color.

The general physical description of those born under this sign is as follows: They are rather tall with a slender, but well-proportioned body, and a ruddy or brownish complexion. Rarely will a Virgo be considered handsome or beautiful by general standards. Their hair is very dark brown or black, and they usually possess short arms and legs. Such individuals will be noted for their shrill, falsetto voice, and sharp facial features.

Virgo's human rule is over the abdomen, bowels, spleen, and the diaphragm or midriff. These people suffer with such things as worms, dysentery, cholic, infirmities of the testicles, vagina problems, depression, derangements of the intestinal canal, and diseases in the abdominal region.

A person born when the first part of *Libra* is rising will have marks (warts or moles) that are soft and hairy, and located near the loins. When the second part of the sign is ascending, these marks will be over towards the center of the stomach. If the third part of Libra was rising at birth, expect the marks to appear in the area just above the genitals.

Libra personifies a well-framed body which is straight and tall. A round face predominates which is rather ruddy and healthy looking, but this is far from beautiful in later years, for pimples and other unpleasant characteristics develop. The eyes are unusually blue, the hair is auburn, smooth, and long.

This sign is presumed to be fruitful and governs the kidneys, loins, and all that region of the body, internal and external. Such health problems as worms, syphilis, feebleness, stones, and ulcers are prominent in such persons.

Scorpio-born persons, whatever the point of ascendancy, will have a dark mole or wart on the belly. Such a mark always indicates misfortune and possible disaster.

Those whose births this sign influences are strongly constructed, robust, and lean to obesity. The face will be broad and square, and the complexion rather dusky, or muddy in appearance. The hair will be curly and dark without much life. The eyes will also be dark and lacking sparkle. Such individuals usually are of middle stature, bow-legged, short-necked, and have hairy bodies. They are active but coarse and uncoordinated in physical movements.

This sign governs the procreative organs and its diseases are those which center around this area, as well as a number of others including such things as kidney stones, gall stones, bladder infections, ruptures, piles, and syphilis and other venereal problems. Injuries to the groin and a grave danger of death from poison or excessive intoxication through alcohol or drugs are prevalent.

Individuals born under the influence of *Sagittarius* will be marked in the area of the thighs, and such warts or moles will be very large and raised. When the first part of this sign is rising at birth, the mark will be on the right thigh. When the second part of the sign is rising, it will be found on the left thigh. Those who have the third part of Sagittarius rising at birth are accordingly marked on the right haunch.

This sign represents those who are tall, well-formed, above middle stature, ruddy complexioned, and with chestnut-colored hair. They have a jovial countenance and are usually found among those who are commonly termed as full of fun. Such persons have a rather long face, and a strong, able body, but they are inclined to baldness.

Those ushered into existence beneath the favorable aspect of Sagittarius are prone to diseases and other illnesses including gout, rheumatism, fevers, and other like problems. They are prone to be hurt through serious falls which could cause fractures in the area of the thighs and buttocks.

Those born under the influence of *Capricorn* will have marks on their knees, the area ruled by this sign. Such warts or moles will be flat and hairless. When the person is born while the first part of this sign is rising, the mark will appear on the right knee.

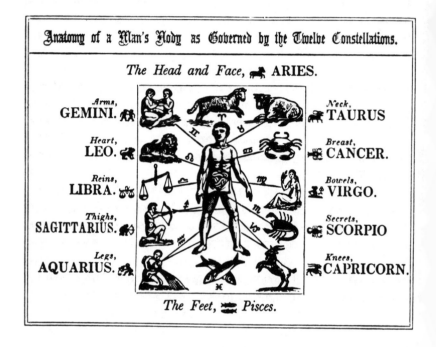

Figure 29

Another fine example of astrological anatomy which shows the supposed connection between the signs of the zodiac and the different portions of the human frame. This appeared in a privately printed work, Mysteries of Astrology, *1854.*

If birth takes place while the second part of the sign is ascending, it will appear on the left knee. Should the third part of Capricorn be rising at the nativity, the mole or wart will be found under one or both of the knees.

It will be remembered that this sign governs the knees alone, and illnesses affecting these individuals will generally affect this area of the body. Capricorn individuals usually have very dry skin, are tall and lean, with a long neck and narrow chest. Their knees will be weak and usually brittle. Such people have dark hair and narrow chins, as well as weak hands.

Diseases and other illnesses affecting the Capricorn people are, disorders of the chest and lungs, skin eruptions, itch and leprosy. Sprains, dislocations, breaks, fractures and other problems incident to the knees are quite common.

The sign of *Aquarius* governs the legs and ankles, therefore, those who are born with this sign ascending in any of its three parts will have its mark (which is a long, pear-shaped mole or wart) on one of the legs, generally in the calf or ankle area. Such a mark denotes extreme inconsistency on the part of the individual.

This sign represents a squat, thick body which leans to plumpness. The face is rather long and the complexion is reddish, but delicate and clear. Such people are quite healthy and they are robust. The hair is sandy or dark flaxen, the eyes hazel, and the teeth are unusually prominent.

Since this sign rules over the legs and ankles of man, the diseases and illnesses pertaining to it generally will be found to affect those parts of the body. Spasmodic and nervous diseases are often quite prevalent, as is lameness, rheumatism and gout. Fractures are also quite common.

The sign of *Pisces* governs the feet, therefore those possessing this sign in their ascending nativity will have moles or warts on their feet. If they were born while the first part of this sign was rising, the flat appearing mole or wart will be found on the right foot. If the second part of Pisces is rising at the time of nativity, a mole or wart will appear on the left foot. If the third part of the sign is ascending, the soles of the feet will be marked, and the heel may well be. If the heel happens to contain such a mark, it assures the person of great honors and dignities throughout life. Such heel marks are usually red and large, and are commonly known as royal marks, a certain sign of distinction.

This sign produces a short, not very well-made body. The face will be round and pale, and such people will be somewhat fleshy. They will tend to stoop with the head pushed far forward while walking. The shoulders will be relatively broad and, generally, they have brown hair. The eyes are brown tinted and the ears are large and protruding.

The diseases and other physical problems encountered through this sign are those pertaining to the feet. Gout is common, as are all forms of lameness and pains incident to those members. Boils and ulcers, anemia, bowel complaints, itch, blotches and mucous discharges are other areas of complaint in general.

We have now described the twelve celestial constellations in regard to each of their physical attributes according to the most highly learned astrologers of the past. Astrology seems to have made very little progress since the days of Claudius Ptolemaeus, who wrote his *Tetrabiblos,* nearly two thousand years ago. This particular work is still widely considered to be the best textbook on the subject in existence today. Modern astrologers, notably Kepler (1571-1638), Galileo (1564-1642), and Descartes (1596-1650), as well as Newton (1642-1727) who was first an astrologer, then an astronomer, have introduced some changes and made new claims. During this period of astrological history, the various planets, as then known, were said to control the following physical ailments:

Uranus causes suicide, mental depression, and sudden and uncommon death. Saturn produces colds, rheumatism, consumption, and many tedious illnesses. Jupiter was found to bring on liver troubles, anemic blood, pleurisy, and sometimes apoplexy—but only in its bad aspects. If this planet were in its

Sign	♄	♃	♂	☉	♀	☿	☽
♈	head breast arms	head throat heart	head bowels eyes	thighs head	reins feet head	secrets legs	knees head
♉	heart breast throat	shoulders belly throat	reins throat neck	knees throat	secrets neck throat	thighs feet	legs throat
♊	belly heart arms	breast reins arms	secrets arms shoulders	legs ankles arms	thighs throat arms	knees head arms	feet shoulders arms
♋	reins belly breast	heart secrets breast	breast stomach thighs	feet breast	arms knees breast	throat legs	head breast stomach
♌	secrets reins heart	thighs belly heart	heart back reins	head heart	breast legs heart.	arms shoulders feet	neck throat heart
♍	thighs secrets bowels	knees reins bowels	bowels legs	neck throat bowels	heart back feet	breast head bowels	arms shoulders bowels
♎	knees thighs reins	legs secrets reins	reins feet	arms shoulders reins	head belly reins	heart back throat	breast reins stomach
♏	legs feet secrets	feet thighs secrets	secrets head	breast stomach secrets	reins throat secrets	belly arms shoulders	secrets heart back
♐	feet legs thighs	head knees thighs	thighs neck throat	heart back thighs	secrets shoulders thighs	reins breast stomach	bowels thighs guts
♑	head feet knees	neck legs knees	knees arms shoulders	bowels guts knees	thighs breasts knees	secrets heart back	reins knees
♒	neck head thighs	arms shoulders legs	legs breast stomach	reins legs	knees heart legs	thighs bowels guts	secrets legs
♓	arms neck feet	breast head feet	feet heart back	secrets feet	legs belly feet	knees reins	thighs feet

Figure 30

A table showing what parts of man's body every planet signifies in the twelve signs. This interesting table was taken from Raphael's Horary Astrology, published in London in 1837.

good aspects, health would certainly be improved. Mars is the cause of fevers, bladder and kidney infections and disorders, ruptures of the blood vessels, smallpox, accidents, burns, scalds, bites, and death through childbirth.

The Sun is said by the ancients to rule the heart, back, arteries, the right eye of man, and the left eye of a woman. Its ailments are disorders of the mouth and throat, a deranged brain, palpitations, fainting spells, weak back and heart, and weak sight.

Venus benefits the health in its good aspects, but otherwise it can produce genital disorders and diseases, problems with the veins, and back disorders.

Mercury is said to preside over the brain, tongue, hands, and feet. Its illnesses and diseases are madness, apoplexy, vertigo, stammering, coughing, rheumatism, gout, fits, and imbecility.

The Moon, when afflicted by evil solar influences, can cause a weakening of the sight, eye blemishes, cancer, madness, female

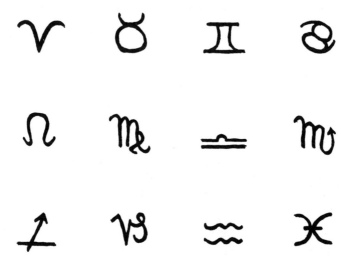

problems, and trouble in the stomach region. In conjunction with the planet Jupiter, it is said to govern the brain, stomach, and the bowels. In such cases, the diseases may also be rheumatism, palsy, gout, smallpox, dropsy, lunacy, and consumption.

BOOK XIII
planetary signatures on the face

Jupiter: Individuals who are born under the powerful influence of Jupiter are noted for their fresh-appearing complexions. Their eyes are large and either blue or grey, with thick, well-formed lids, and long, attractive lashes. Their hair, usually chestnut, or brown, is crisp and curly. They generally have well defined and somewhat arched eyebrows. The nose of the Jupiter person is straight and somewhat fleshy, with a slight rise or arch. Ears are generally medium in size and lie rather close to the head. Seldom will a Jupiter's ears be seen to protrude. Their cheeks are firm but fleshy with mildly defined bones. A large mouth with generous, full, and curved lips is evident, and the upper lip projects over the lower. Teeth are also rather large but the two front teeth are larger than the rest. A large dimpled chin can readily be noted. The men born under this planet's influence tend to lose their hair early in life. Although they eventually may get bald, they are often seen with curly, very thick, brownish beards.

Mars: People born under the influence of the planet Mars tend to possess a short and rather square-shaped head, small but with a receding hairline on a high forehead. A rounded face that is often squared off at the bottom is evident, as well as dry, tough, rather reddened skin, especially around the ears. The organs of hearing most often appear to be large and long, set high on the head and although relatively straight, they stand away or project from it. The eyes are large, round, and wide open which makes these individuals appear to be somewhat credulous, yet they have a fierce, fixed stare. The whites often seem to be somewhat bloodshot. Short, very bushy eyebrows are a trademark of the Mars people, and they are placed very close to the eye itself, usually stopping midway over the eyes. Several short, vertical wrinkles are to be seen between the brows. A large mouth with a rather thin, compressed-appearing upper lip is common, as is a short, hooked, eaglelike nose with dilated nostrils. The chin is extremely large and projecting, with a strongly developed jaw, and the cheeks are somewhat hollowed with well-defined cheekbones. The hair color is red or sandy, somewhat coarse and quite curly. Men born under Mars are quite capable of growing a very thick beard which will be the same fiery color as the hair. People with such thick, reddish-colored hair are always found to be hot-tempered and very courageous. The hair will usually be found to be redder at the temples and just over the ears, as well as on the beard. It signifies an abundant energy and constant activity, unless, that is, the other Mars characteristics do not show up in the features. This type of hair strengthens the force of personality, and as a direct result, it adds power in musical composition, gives more color sense to those in art, and brings eloquence to authors and poets.

Mercury: Individuals born under the influence of the planet Mercury usually will be seen to possess long faces with delicate, mobile features. They have a very fine skin texture, which is honey-colored and soft, almost silky feeling. Such people are highly intuitive, very easily excited, and extremely nervous, therefore their skin changes in tint with each change of emotion. They, too, have hair of a reddish hue, more of a brown than golden, or what might be called auburn. Their hair is very fine and is noted for its suppleness. Persons with such hair are ardent and vivacious, if, with this type of hair, they also possess hazel eyes. Such a combination is a definite signature of Mercury, and it indicates a keen intelligence, a natural faculty for study, and an excellent memory. On the other hand, these people are also noted for their selfishness and cruelty. A high and prominent forehead, and long delicate eyebrows which lie very close over the eyes are other Mercury clues. Such brows are the highly mobile type which seem to move up and down with every emotion. The eyes, mentioned previously, appear to be somewhat sunken, quick-moving or restless, with a yellowish tint to the whites. The lids appear to be rather thin and never are seen to droop over the eyes. The ears are delicate and long, with more color than the ears of those born under the influence of the Sun. A long straight nose with delicate nostrils, a rounded tip, and a faintly perceptible dimple at the extreme end, is commonly found in Mercury people. Although the face is quite long, it is generally oval in shape, full at the temples, and gently curving down to a long, pointed chin which projects at the lip. The mouth is also rather delicate and it tends to droop a little at each corner. The lips are quite thin, unexpressive, and usually held slightly apart. The upper lip tends to project more than does the lower lip, and it is slightly thicker. The teeth are always quite small and very straight and even. Mercury people are often extremely attractive since they possess classical beauty.

Moon: Many individuals possessing vivid imaginations are born under the influence of this planet. Their heads are basically quite round with very broad temples and a full forehead above the eyebrows. Although the forehead is broad, it is also quite low, and it falls back or retreats near the top. These people have soft skin, and an almost colorless, pale complexion. The hair is fine, soft, and ash-colored, never very thick, and rather lifeless. This usually denotes those who are rather lazy and dreamy by nature. Persons with this kind of hair combined with blue-grey eyes, and eyelashes that appear to be straight, long, and light in color, with eyebrows that are blonde and not well defined, are often depressive, changeable, and slow to start things. Women with this skin and hair tend to be very romantic, and make devoted lovers and wives. They are incapable and unwilling to exert themselves, and have little or no perseverance. Their generosity is only in words—not in deeds. The face of those born under the predominating lunar influence is generally large and round with a small, short, and round-tipped nose. The eyes generally will be found to be the same color as the hair, and set close together. Such people have small mouths with full, open, and pouting lips, which have a very pale coloring. The teeth are most often irregular and quite large, while the ears are rounded, medium-sized, very pale, close to the head, and set in a sloping direction. The chin is round, somewhat retreating, and rather fleshy. If such a person happens to have been born while the Moon is in an eclipse, blindness may often result.

Saturn: Persons born under the dominating influence of this melancholy planet will be seen to have little coloring in their faces. The skin will tend to be rather dusky, or have a yellow or ashen-grey tint. All Saturnians have eyebrows that meet between the eyes, a characteristic signifying jealousy, suspicion, and deeply passionate natures. A nose that bends downward, with a fine, sharp tip is one of Saturn's signatures; this denotes a sad or gloomy disposition and a natural wit. Combined, these traits often lead to cynicism. Voltaire had such a nose. The mouth of the Saturn-born individual has a projecting lower lip, a sign of strong distrust. Should the under lip be very full as well as projecting, and if it tends to droop limply in a way that exposes the teeth, it indicates a highly sensual nature. There is always a danger that these individuals will go to extremes in order to satisfy the gross pleasures of their senses. Of course, an intellectual brow and a firm, energetic nose would lessen the evil of this sign. Very large ears are also a signature of Saturn. The overall ugliness of those ruled by this planet can be mitigated to a large degree by the influence of other planets. For example, the union of Venus and Jupiter will produce beauty of a rather serious and melancholic sort. A great number of strikingly beautiful Spanish and Italian faces show the results of the combined influence of these planets.

Sun: Persons born under the dominating influence of the Sun usually will be found to have well-proportioned, evenly balanced features, and a rather soft, pliable, yellowish-tinted skin. Although their skin is somewhat sallow in appearance, they will have color in their cheeks and lips. The hair generally is golden with a reddish tint, or a very bright, deeply rich-looking gold. It is crisp and very wavy, growing thick and low on the forehead. Such a head of hair indicates an artistic and poetic temperament, and these individuals will be ardently fond of poetry, music, painting, or some other form of artistic expression. Both sexes possess an abundance of intuitiveness. They do not logically reason things out—they "feel" or sense them. They have a spontaneous temper, but are quickly calmed after an outburst, and usually seem to be in an optimistic mood. Their eyebrows are light, but, still well defined. Golden brown or greenish eyes predominate and these are sparkling and nicely shaped. The eyelashes are darker than the hair, but still quite light and they can easily be traced in a long sweeping line to the temples. The ears are medium-sized, pale, rather long, close to the sides of the head, and the lobes are fleshy and pink. Weak sight is common in those who were born during an eclipse of the Sun. The chin is quite prominent, round, but not at all fleshy. The cheeks are full, but not plump nor fleshy, and the bones are not noticeable. The jaw is long and oval and the teeth are even, but somewhat off-white. A moderate-sized mouth is evident and nicely formed. The lips meet evenly, and neither the upper nor the lower project.

Venus: Those individuals who are born under the dominant influence of this powerful planet greatly resemble those under the realm of Jupiter, except for the fact that their beauty is much more feminine in nature. The white, delicate, finely tinted skin tone is similar to that of Jupiterians, but the Venus-endowed skin is still finer in texture, softer to the touch, and more transparent. Venus people have rounded faces and the cheek- and jawbones do not show in the least as they do in Jupiterians. Dimples ornament their softly rounded cheeks, as well as their mildly prominent chin and corner of the mouth. The mouth itself is small with full, very red lips. The lower lip is usually slightly fuller, and the right side of this lower lip is larger than the left. A mouth of this type, was said by the ancients to represent ardour in lovemaking, and a general sensuousness. A wart just above the upper lip shows a coarse and very cruel nature, while a mole in the same area denotes a strong attraction for the opposite sex. Their hair is long, thick, very soft, and light brown. Both sexes with such hair are lovers of all things beautiful, and they intensely dislike quarrels and discord. Men, though, tend to be somewhat effeminate, and extremely emotional. This often shows itself in the ease with which such men are led to tears. Venus foreheads are oval in shape, rather low, and meshed with a series of fine veins. The eyes are noted for their distinctive qualities. They are bluish-white, almost transparent, large, clear, and somewhat moist in appearance. The pupils are usually quite large in proportion to the whites, which tend to be limpid. The eyelids are well formed, very thin skinned, and have delicate azure veins on them. The eyebrows are darker than is the hair, and they sweep in a delicate line, but they do not meet at the nose. Small, thin and rounded ears, tinted a light pink, and very close to the head, are always signs of Venus. The nose is broad at its base between the eyes, and it is straight, and rather rounded at the tip. Such a nose often appears to be slightly upturned; they are never bent downwards towards the mouth. The nostrils are round, but dilated and very flexible. All Venus people have white, small, even teeth, which are firmly set in coral tinted gums.

Planetary Combinations: Although the planetary signs described in the above apply only to that one particular planet, it is a rarity for anyone to be born under the direct influence of a single body. Seldom will you ever see a face that has the pure signs of any one planet by itself. Mixtures are most common, for, more often than not, a person is born under the powerful influences of two or more planets. It is up to the physiognomist to examine and then ascertain which is the dominant planet.

An example of planetary mixtures is that which occurs as a result of a Saturn-Jupiter union. Such people will be seen to have pale skin lacking freshness and vitality. The hair and eyes will be chestnut, and the face will be oval in shape.

Very hot-tempered people, if they have blue eyes, will also have tints of green in them and, when angered, a sudden red fleck of light appears in them. Such individuals were born under the duo influence of Jupiter-Mars. The red tint of anger indicates that of the two planets, Mars dominates with no small degree of authority.

A union of Saturn and the Moon produces eyes with weakly marked brows, and very thin lashes which are devoid of any upward curve. Such brows and lashes denote physical weakness and a melancholy disposition. The eyes themselves are usually either a pale, rather colorless blue tint, or a dull black that lacks sparkle.

A union of Venus with the Sun produces a beautiful complexion, rich golden-brown or chestnut hair, full and bright brown eyes with long, distinctive lashes, a delicately formed nose, and a beautiful, sensual mouth. "Women born under the double influence of Venus and the Sun," says an old Italian astrologer, "are loving, lovely, and beloved." All persons born under such a combination are charming, but extremely inconsistent. They are full of affection and tenderness, and they are ardently artistic. They are extremely impressionable, and tend to love readily, and then, as readily, forget. Their emotional feelings are quick, but not often very deep and lasting.

A Venus-Saturn union produces thick, black, crisp and curling hair, as opposed to the hair of a true Saturnian, which tends to be thin and straight. When these two planets are united, they give more force to the character of the individual. The natural warmth and impulsiveness of Venus is tempered by the general distrust of Saturn. Prudence is the end result and, usually, success will follow.

BOOK XIV
SOLAR HOROSCOPES:
female

The following horoscopes, as well as those covering men, in Book XV, are translations from an ancient Hebrew manuscript which was found near Cairo, in 1836, at the time of the removal of the obelisk to France.

Aquarius: The woman who is born under the influence of this sign will have a charming and very expressive face. She will be unable to hide her true emotional feelings. She will be highly romantic and slightly depressive by nature. She will marry well, and happiness will be hers. A serious illness will strike at the age of fifty, but through the affectionate care of her husband, she will completely recover, and then live on to a ripe old age. She will be surrounded by many grandchildren and will experience much bliss in the advancing years of her life.

Figure 31

Aquarius—January 21 to February 19; Pisces—February 20 to March 20; Aries—March 21 to April 19; Taurus—April 20 to May 20; Gemini—May 21 to June 21; Cancer—June 22 to July 21; Leo—July 22 to August 21; Virgo—August 22 to September 22; Libra—September 23 to October 22; Scorpio—October 23 to November 21; Sagittarius—November 22 to December 21; Capricorn—December 22 to January 20.

Pisces: The woman who is born under the influence of this sign will be fairly attractive, and she will have a good disposition. Although she will be kind and thoughtful around those in need, she will also be self-indulgent. Her love for luxury will influence every phase of her life. She will marry at least two times and will bear many healthy children. The stars do not really promise such a woman much enduring happiness. She will become very ill in her fifties. This may require serious surgery, but recovery is certain. Death will finally come about the age of sixty-eight, and it will be very quick.

Aries: The woman born under the influence of this sign will be quick-tempered, strong-willed, very brave, and quite selfish. She will marry at twenty-three, but will not wed happily. Very few children will be born, and those that are will be weak and somewhat sickly. She will be a widow at about the age of forty, and will marry a second time within a year of her husband's passing. No man will be able to bring her true happiness, and much of this will be due to her own greed. She will suddenly die at the age of fifty-six due to an accident.

Taurus: The woman born under the influence of this sign will be noted for her gracefulness and her well-proportioned, highly stimulating physical attributes. She will have impeccable manners and will attract many of the opposite sex. She will run great risks both from water and fire, and will have problems with her sight. Her eyes will grow weaker in advancing age, so much so that she will deeply fear blindness, but this problem will eventually be overcome. Many lovers are hers, but she will marry one time only. She will be survived by her mate and many children. She is destined to die before the age of sixty.

Gemini: The woman born under the influence of this sign will be extremely fluent in both speech and writing. She will also be noted for her gracious manners, her wit and intelligence, and her sensitivity. For these reasons she will be loved dearly by many of both sexes. She will finally marry at twenty-five, as a virgin, but she will not love her husband as he does her. She will have very few children and these will not live beyond childhood. She herself will meet death at the age of sixty-six.

Cancer: The woman born under the influence of this sign will be fond of luxury and will be somewhat lazy. She will never contribute much of anything in her lifetime. She will eat and drink to the extent of being considered a glutton. She will no doubt marry young, but many disagreements will mar this relationship, most points of friction being caused by her own infidelity. She will eventually marry at least three times, and her last husband will be the most suitable for her. Several children will be born, but each will be rather sickly. She will have a number of serious illnesses in later years; one, at seventy, will end her unhappy life. Only through death will such a woman solve all her problems.

Leo: The woman born under the influence of this sign will be very charming with a pretty face. Her figure will be proportioned beautifully, and her expression will be agreeable. Her voice will be one of her charms, and she will be admired for her wit, musical capabilities, and her dancing prowess. She will have fairly good health throughout life. Many men will seek her hand in marriage, but none will be found acceptable until she reaches the age of twenty-two. She will have many lovers, but no serious men in her life until this time. Her husband will love her dearly, and this feeling will be gratefully returned. She will be inclined toward religious activities and will educate her children in this aspect of life. Death will greet her at the age of about sixty-nine.

Virgo: The woman born under the influence of this sign will possess a quick temper. She will be most difficult for anyone to please under any circumstances. She will be fond of sexual pleasures as well as all others in life, and she will be ambitious to climb socially. This great desire to be known, accepted, and admired, will cause others to speak maliciously of her. She will marry early, but will lose her husband in his youth. She will marry again very soon after widowhood. Neither husband will be made very happy, for her actions will create jealousy. She will suffer with a multitude of illnesses caused by anemia. A serious sickness will strike at the age of forty-eight, but she will survive and live another fifteen years. Her life will be in constant turmoil, full of anxieties, and loaded with insurmountable troubles.

Libra: The woman born under the influence of this sign will be cheerful at all times, and noted for her kindess to others. She will be a lively person and will love music and art, in both of which she will excel. Many men will love such a woman for her amiable attitudes and her feminine appearance. Marriage will come twice: the first to a wealthy, mature man, the second to a younger man, who will waste her financial resources. She will lead a gay, pleasure-filled life, and will flirt extensively. This will be a source of displeasure to her husband, for she will tend to have many love affairs right before his eyes. She will have a weakness for gambling and will lose much money in this manner. This and her love life will bring on much discomfort and anxiety in later years.

Scorpio: The woman born under the influence of this sign will be extremely sensitive to the feelings of others, and she will have a friendly, outgoing nature. Many of both sexes will enjoy her company, but she will be inclined to be overly fond of partaking of pleasure with men. She will be loved and admired by relatives who will not know about her well-hidden desires and secret affairs. Yet, she will make a good wife, for she will be energetic in the discharge of all household duties. A temper is evident, as is a revengeful nature. She will experience much trouble from lawsuits in her youthful years, most of these involving a man's wife. She need not fear the results of such suits for luck is on her side. She will marry once, after her twenty-sixth year, and will die at about sixty-eight. She will have no children by legitimate means.

Sagittarius: The woman born under the influence of this sign is unable to take criticism, has a bad temper, is irritable, and very timid. She has a high intellect, and will be faithful in her love and friendship. She is generous with her affections, but will reserve her chastity for her husband. Marriage will come after twenty, and many children will be born. Suffering will be caused by the vicious tongues of supposed friends who talk to her husband behind her back. Malicious gossip will be spread in this manner, but her innocence will prevail and finally be made known. In the end she will be fully exonerated of all falsehoods. She will live to at least sixty-eight.

Capricorn: The woman born under the influence of this sign will be of an agreeable nature, kind, thoughtful, and well liked by everyone she meets. She will marry twice. The first husband will be poor, but he will love her with devotion. He will be respected for his straightforwardness. Her second mate will be wealthier than the first, but not as affectionate. He will be more inclined to seek the charms of other women. She will suffer much from depression and, at the age of thirty, mental illness will strike. She will completely recover and then live until she is forty-seven.

BOOK XV
SOLAR HOROSCOPES:
MALE

Aquarius: The man born under the influence of this sign will be optimistic, happy, of a lively disposition, and an excellent speaker. He will achieve whatever it is he desires most in life, and is destined for fame within the bounds of his own country. He will be subject to gloom and depression, will be very religiously oriented, and of a highly conscientious nature. The stars, however, portend that he must pass through a period of poverty in youth, as well as a multitude of other problems including the deaths of some close relatives and friends. Such tragedies will come prior to the age of thirty. He will do much traveling, and will suffer some serious illness. Women will influence him to his detriment, and he will lose his first wife. But, he will marry again, the second being very unfortunate. Illness will again strike at the age of thirty, but recovery is seen, and he will live on to about sixty-four years of age.

Pisces: The man who is born under the influence of this sign will be good-natured, full of kindness, and rather jolly. He will be very fond of water sports, and take great delight in fishing. He will not be very studious, for perseverance is lacking, but he will follow orders well and he will perform his duties when given the necessary instructions. He will be rather reserved and will seem slow in offering his personal opinions about any subject. He will be deeply influenced by females because of his deep-rooted passions and love of luxury. He will practice great economy in living expenses, including household items. Money will be freely utilized on personal pleasures outside the family circle. He will enjoy traveling and will experience more good fortune in areas other than his home country. He will be rather ingenious and respected for his ability to understand the problems of others. His advice will always be wise, and it is better for others than himself. He will lose his wife quite early in life, but he will not marry again. This will be due to laziness rather than to a lack of feeling for another woman.

Aries: The man born under the influence of this sign will be a loud talker, very warm-blooded regarding women, and a heavy eater. He will be fond of all sports, especially those of the field type, and he will be noted for his great courage. He will be subject to many accidents throughout life that will most often be caused by fires or by four-footed beasts. He will be unreliable in his affections, and will be found to suffer much from his capricious affairs with those of the opposite sex. He will grow wiser with age in this respect, but he will never marry. Poverty and illness may strike around the age of fifty, and this will cause him to become alienated from the friends of his youth. His life will not be prolonged much beyond the age of fifty-five.

Taurus: The man born under the influence of this sign will be fierce and very cruel. He will be extremely fond of the opposite sex, but they will not like him very much. As a consequence, he will suffer deeply. He will be ambitious and will experience great luck in all business endeavors. He will tend to cause trouble because of his uninhibited talkativeness, and will never seem to be very prudent. He will marry a wealthy woman, and will receive other money through legacies from relatives. Illness of a serious nature will strike him around the age of forty, but he will survive this, and will eventually recover completely. Riches will come soon after this sickness. His life will continue until about the age of sixty-two, and at that time, he will die of the same illness which he experienced at forty.

Gemini: The man born under the influence of this sign will be very well liked for his amiable disposition, and he will raise his family well. He will be subject to ulcers and skin diseases. He will do much foreign traveling and will acquire many beautiful things as a result. He will be noted for his attentiveness to those of the opposite sex, and will be gracious, valiant, conscientious, and a perfect gentleman at all times. He will be bitten by a poisonous snake, but will recover after a long period of suffering. He will be falsely accused of some serious action and imprisonment is destined. He will eventually emerge victorious and his innocence will be widely acknowledged. His marriage status is uncertain.

Cancer: The man born under the influence of this sign will be noted for his deceitful ways with those of the opposite sex. He will make a practice of being unfaithful to his lovers, and cannot be trusted at his word. Yet, he will be extremely popular with women because of his gracious manners, and his ability to smooth their ruffled feelings with much diplomacy. He will travel extensively and, through this, will suffer from many accidents. He will lose almost everything in middle age because of the misconduct of his relatives. They will, through extravagance, spend all of their father's money, and then come to the Cancer brother for more. He will, through deep sympathy, give them all he possesses. He will be successful in farming or some other allied field. He will end his life with some serious illness at about forty-eight.

Leo: The man born under the influence of this sign will be hot-tempered, talkative, somewhat boastful, and a bore to many. But, most people will tend to like him because of his pleasant outlook and jovial nature. He will admire women deeply, but will be extremely inconsistent in his feelings of love and affection. He will marry one time, but this will not be to the woman he loves the most. His courage is great and he fears no danger of any kind. He is rather proud and will succeed at almost any undertaking.

Virgo: The man born under the influence of this sign will be ambitious, enterprising, and very honorable. His weakness will be an inherent changeableness that will cause alarm in a crisis. He is destined to suffer many illnesses, and he will be menaced by death or a life in prison around the age of thirty; yet, he will eventually escape both of these evils. He will feel deeply sympathetic toward those of the opposite sex, and will be benevolent to those he cares for. His counsel will be heeded by his friends. He will have a very beautiful wife who will be the envy of friends and foes alike. This woman he will deeply and sincerely love, but she will not return his affections.

Libra: The man born under the influence of this sign will be extremely fluent, but he will sound angry even when he is not. He will be highly thought of by friends and men in high positions for his prudence and advice. Great respect will be commanded from all those who know or hear of him. He will be noted for his fairness and many honorable qualities and he will be conscientious in all dealings with fellow human beings. He is destined to marry at least twice. The second wife will come after forty, and she will turn out to be extravagant and a troublemaker. She will spend all his savings and will bring on his death before he is sixty.

Scorpio: The man born under the influence of this sign will be ungraceful in his movements, and unreliable in all dealings. He will be prompt in coming to conclusions and in giving advice, but inconsistency will tend to make others shun him. He will promise one thing and end up doing another. His word will not be dependable, and those who do have dealings with him will eventually lose all confidence. They will soon learn that this man will be certain to deceive them. He will have a bad temper and many rather perverse ways of punishing those who cross him. Many enemies will be made in a lifetime and, notwithstanding his wily ways, he will end up broke. He will travel extensively and will be somewhat of a vagabond. He will probably not ever marry, and will, in all probability, die violently.

Sagittarius: The man born under the influence of this sign will be prudent, thrifty, and very studious. He will travel and see most foreign nations, and he will make much money while quite youthful. This will create much envy in his friends. A close relative will try to prejudice others against him, but this will not be very successful, for he will be well received and very popular socially. He will be generous with all friends, but many will take advantage of this. He will persevere and attain a high position in whatever he decides to undertake as a profession. He will suffer internal illnesses, but will overcome them all and live to a ripe old age. He will marry, have several children, and be a generous father; but he will not remain faithful to his wife. She, in turn, will never know of his affairs. His children will be spoiled, and as a result, will be ungrateful to him.

Capricorn: The man born under the influence of this sign will greatly admire those of the opposite sex, and much of his life will be governed by their whims of fancy. He will love luxury so much that this could lead to his downfall. He is likely to be bitten by some mad animal and will be menaced by many illnesses of the eyes. He will be deceived by a woman who will be the cause of much injury and anxiety.

BOOK XVI
SOLAR HOROSCOPES:
CHILDREN

One area of astrological prediction that should be studied with a great deal of care and accuracy, is that covering the forecasting of a baby's life. In India, the moment of birth is observed with the greatest vigilance, and it is anxiously timed on three separate clocks to insure total accuracy. Then, immediately upon the completion of birth, an astrologer is paid to compute the child's horoscope.

Many of us do not know at exactly what moment we were born, and, therefore, we cannot be absolutely certain that our own horoscope will be right. Most reputable astrologers agree that we should take necessary steps to see that the next generation is not burdened with such a handicap. Given the exact moment of birth, it is claimed that all of life's many aspects may be studied with much more certainty of success.

Figure 32

The clock dial and the zodiac are one. The zodiac is a circle of 360 degrees divided like a clock dial into twelve parts. While the zodiac is broken down into degrees, minutes, and seconds, the clock dial is divided into twelve parts or hours, minutes, and seconds.

The following solar horoscopes are of a general nature, and can be utilized to determine the good and evil influences on the fortune of children born under each of the signs of the zodiac.

Aquarius: This sign rules from the 21st of January to the 19th of February. The child born under its influence will have one leg slightly larger than the other, either in length or in width. A very quick temper will be evident, but this should be offset by a rather buoyant, cheerful attitude in general. These children are extremely changeable in disposition. They will have the distinct advantage of being articulate and very fluent in dealing with others. This trait is further strengthened by prudence and a keen mentality as well as natural shrewdness and material wealth. The health of such children will be quite delicate, and they will be subject to much illness and possible disease. Their most perilous years will be at the ages of thirty-five, forty-two, and eighty.

Pisces: The sign of the *fishes* governs from the 20th of February to the 20th of March. The child born under its influence will have a rather large chest, a small head, long face, light skin, rounded eyes, and a cold, impassive nature. Such children will often appear to be very sluggish in movements and may seem to be apathetic about things around them, in general. They will seem rather somber, and are destined to meet with many unusual struggles during their youthful years. But age will bring wealth for most of these children, and they should be quite well-to-do in the long run. Many excellent qualities of leadership are inherent. Their most perilous years will be at the ages of fifteen, thirty, and thirty-eight.

Aries: The *ram* rules from the 21st of March to the 19th of April. The child born under the influence of this sign will have a heavy crop of dark hair, hair which may appear to be woolly. Such children will be endowed with rather small ears, and a long neck. They will have a fiery disposition, but this will be tempered by an excellent sense of judgment and fair play. Talents will be best suited in the teaching profession, but some undertaking which would include a great deal of traveling is most desirable. These children are natural matchmakers, and therefore will often be invaluable as close friends. Their most perilous years will be at the ages of twelve, thirty, and thirty-five.

Taurus: The dominion of the *bull* lasts from the 20th of April to the 20th of May. The child born under the influence of this sign will have a broad, very high forehead, a long face, and chestnut-colored hair. A rather somber, depressed temperament will be strongly in evidence, but such children try hard always to be friendly toward others, and they are quick to grant favors asked of them. An inclination to overeat must be watched carefully. As these children grow and mature, little interest is shown in business enterprises. They become more reserved with age, and will surely be the victim of jealousy on more than one occasion. Much care should be given during times of illness. Little or no medicine should be given, and a change of air will do most to restore the child's health. The most dangerous years for children born under the bull are the ages of twelve, twenty-two, thirty-two, fifty, and seventy-four.

Gemini: The *twins* rule from the 21st of May to the 21st of June. The child born under this sign will have a large chest and a well-proportioned body which will be of medium stature. Such children will be faithful to their parents and other members of the family, will have an affectionate and loving temperament, and feel generous toward others. They will do their utmost to bring happiness and to give pleasure to others. Good health and fortune is destined, and the child will have an inclination for mathematics. The dangerous periods in the life of such children are at the ages of nine, ten, fifteen, twenty-five, thirty-three, and forty-two.

Cancer: The *crab* dominates from the 22nd of June to the 21st of July. The child born under the influence of this sign will be short in stature, but will possess long limbs. The shoulders will be very broad and the eyes will be rather small, almost beady in appearance. Such children are basically cold and withdrawn by nature, and have an inclination to be somewhat effeminate in their actions. They are rather serious-minded, opinionated, and awkward in conversation. They are often contemptuous around their elders, feel a great deal of pride in themselves, and are greedy. The most perilous years for such a child will be at the ages of four, fourteen, twenty-four, and thirty-seven.

Leo: The *lion* rules from the 22nd of July to the 21st of August. Children born under this sign's influence will have a broad chest, a large chin, a penetrating stare, and upper limbs that are larger than the lower ones. Such a child will be a very fast runner, have excellent coordination, and will be gracefully proportioned. Good judgment and a mild-mannered temperament will be evident. Seldom will they throw temper tantrums. They are affectionate and generally optimistic about everything. The dangerous years will be at the ages of twelve, sixteen, nineteen, thirty-nine, and forty-seven.

Virgo: The sign of the *virgin* governs from the 22nd of August to the 22nd of September. Children born under the influence of this sign will be endowed with many fine qualities, splendid talents, and a well-proportioned body. Such children often feels sadness and seems easily depressed over little things. They never lie and try to deceive parents or guardians, but are never ones to show much of an outward display of affection. Though rather effeminate in actions, they are very sincere, and will not viciously try to hurt anyone. These little ones are willing to conform to all rules and will be noted for their obedience. No medicines should be taken during the period of this sign. The most perilous years of such a child will be at the ages of sixteen, eighteen, forty-two, and sixty-five.

Libra: The *balance,* or *scales,* governs from the 23rd of September to the 22nd of October. Children born under the influence of this sign will be attractive. They are of medium height, and possess a tawny complexion, with a handsome face. They are endowed with the gift of eloquence, and have a natural singing voice which, with proper training, could be the envy of most professionals. Such children are deeply affected by the misfortune of others and usually go out of their way to assist in a time of need. The perilous years of this child will be at the ages of thirteen, fifteen, twenty-eight, and eighty-five.

Scorpio: The *scorpion* rules from the 23rd of October to the 21st of November. The infants born under its auspices will be short and very broad, quite hairy, rather handsome in countenance, and will have large hands and feet. They will walk quickly, and will have to be disciplined often for fighting among friends. They seem to be warlike by nature, and therefore are continually in some sort of trouble. Such children will be noticed for their intensity of feeling, and for seemingly foolish or unthinking actions. Their disposition is extremely changeable. No internal medicines should be given them during the sign's reign. The most dangerous years will be at the ages of ten, fourteen, sixteen, forty-three, and sixty-six.

Sagittarius: The *archer* rules from the 22nd of November to the 21st of December. Children born under the influence of this sign will be pale in complexion with large arms and legs, a long face, and light blonde, straggly hair. Their disposition is affectionate but quick to anger. Absolutely no medicines should be taken during the archer's rule. The most perilous days in the life of such a child are at the ages of eight, nine, ten, eleven, twenty-eight, and eighty-nine.

Capricorn: The *goat* governs from the 22nd of December to the 20th of January. Children born under the influence of this sign will have slender legs, a lean body, and will be subject to pain in the knees as well as headaches. They will often feel rejected and gloomy and will find it difficult to get along well

Figure 33

From Witness of the Stars, *privately published by the Reverend Ethelbert W. Bullinger in 1893.*

with relatives because of a contrary nature. All types of medicines may be safely taken during the reign of this sign. The most dangerous years will be at the ages of eight, eleven, eighteen, thirty-two, and seventy-seven.

BOOK XVII
ASTROLOGICAL
MARRIAGE TIPS

It is a well-known fact that the strong and handsome young people of the ancient Egyptian and Babylonian cultures were said to be the result of consulting the astrologers of that day prior to entering into the bonds of matrimony. The pages that follow will reveal a number of the astrological beliefs that were extensively practiced at that time in an effort to produce harmonious and productive marriages.

Some exceptions to these signs, will, of course, be found, yet, it is safe to predict happy marriages eight out of ten times. According to the experience of the ages, most couples who have married in accordance with the rules of astrology will be happy, and most unfortunate marriages are of those people who were united contrary to these signs. Compatible partners may be found in the following periods of birth:

December 22 to January 20th: Any persons born between these dates are under the sign of Capricorn. They have a burning desire for knowledge. They will not be happy working for others, but will do well by themselves. They are entertaining and enjoy telling amusing stories.

These people should always select their closest friends and marriage partners from persons born under the sign of Taurus, from April 20 to May 20; Virgo, from August 22 to September 22; or Libra, from September 23 to October 22.

January 21 to February 19: Any persons born between these dates are under the sign of Aquarius. They possess magnetic personalities, and are able to learn with little or no apparent effort and study. They are good about asking for advice, but terrible when it comes to abiding by it. They are often depressed, but then optimistic.

These people should always select their closest friends and marriage partners from persons born under the sign of Aries, from March 21 to April 19; or from people born under the sign of Sagittarius, from November 22 to December 21.

February 20 to March 20: Any persons born between the above dates are under the sign of Pisces. They are fond of nature's natural beauty, and they tend to love all art forms. They cannot see dishonesty in others, and often spend much time in meditation and worry.

These people should always select their closest friends and marriage partners from persons born under the sign of Virgo, from August 22 to September 22; Capricorn, from December 22 to January 20; or from their own sign.

March 21 to April 19: Any persons born between these dates are under the sign of Aries. They are best noted for their energy and ambition. These people require much sleep. They are extremely fond of elegance, and they usually possess a great deal of leadership ability.

These people should always select their closest friends and marriage partners from persons born under the sign of Sagittarius, from November 22 to December 21; or from their own sign.

April 20 to May 20: Any person born between these dates is under the sign of Taurus. They are extremely generous with their finances, and love parties and social activities among friends. Many of these people are leaders in reform movements and political bodies.

These people should always select their closest friends and marriage partners from persons born under the sign of Capricorn, December 22 to January 20; or from people born under the sign of Libra, September 23 to October 22.

May 21 to June 21: Any persons born between these dates are under the sign of Gemini. They are rather excitable people, extremely sensitive, and range from cheerfulness to a feeling of despair or gloom. They should make a sincere study of all faults and then remedy them.

These people should always select their closest friends and marriage partners from persons born under the sign of Aquarius, January 20 to February 19; or from people born under the sign of Virgo, August 22 to September 22.

June 22 to July 21: Any persons born between these dates are under the sign of Cancer. They are extremely fond of showy clothing, travel, and a change of scenery. They possess a strong determination, well developed intuition, and leadership capabilities.

These people should always select their closest friends and marriage partners from persons born under the sign of Pisces, February 20 to March 20; or from people born under the sign of Scorpio, October 23 to November 21.

July 22 to August 21: Any persons born between these dates are under the sign of Leo. They have a wonderful sense of

Figure 34

The story of the New Testament related in the astrological sense. Note the birth of Christ under Capricorn, his baptism under Aquarius, etc. From Stowe's Bible Astrology, *privately printed, 1907.*

intuition, and are extremely emotional. They are exceptionally well-balanced individuals who attempt to create happiness in the rest of society.

These people should always select their closest friends and marriage partners from persons born under the sign of Aries, March 21 to April 19; Sagittarius, November 22 to December 21; or Libra, September 23 to October 22.

August 22 to September 22: Any persons born between these dates are under the sign of Virgo. They have magnetic personalities, and seem to excel in musical lines. They make excellent designers, are generous, loyal, and creative. They take great interest in the love problems and affairs of their acquaintances.

These people should always select their closest friends and marriage partners from persons born under their own sign, Virgo.

September 23 to October 22: Any persons born between these dates are under the sign of Libra. These people have an abundance of excess energy, are very ambitious, and are the most friendly of all the signs. They feel a great repulsion and horror over bloodshed and love animals.

These people should always select their closest friends and marriage partners from persons born under the sign of Sagittarius, November 22 to December 21; Aquarius, January 21 to February 19; or from their own sign.

October 23 to November 21: Any persons born between these dates are under the sign of Scorpio. These people are prone to be quite suspicious, but they are still very friendly. They possess great tact, and have an excellent command of the language. Their willpower is strong.

These people should always select their closest friends and marriage partners from persons born under the sign of Virgo, August 22 to September 22; Pisces, February 20 to March 20; or from people born under the sign of Libra, September 23 to October 22.

November 22 to December 21: Any persons born between these dates are under the sign of Sagittarius. They are neat and orderly by nature, and extremely cautious when it comes to spending or investing money. They are generally more successful when relying on their own judgment.

These people should always select their closest friends and marriage partners from persons born under the sign of Aquarius, January 21 to February 19; Aries, March 21 to April 19; or from their own sign.

BOOK XVIII
GENERAL ASPECTS
OF EACH ZODIACAL SIGN

Aries ♈ (Mars ♂)

The Sign of the Ram

March 21 to April 19

Aries, termed by the ancients "the house of Mars" and exaltation of the Sun, is the first northern sign of the zodiac. It is a dry, masculine, fiery, eastern, choleric, and violent sign. It belongs to the fiery triplicity along with Leo and Sagittarius. The general disposition will be toward violence, haste, and intemperance. A nativity under this sign denotes a lack of caution and fearlessness to a degree that might endanger the individual's life through reckless actions, if, that is, the power of the sign is not counterbalanced by the aspects of the more favorable planets. For example, a favorable appearance of Mercury or of the Moon will have a decided influence for good upon the destinies which they indicate—and their unfavorable position will add materially to the evil influences of the more malignant planetary signs.

Every sign among the constellations governs certain divisions of the globe—physically, politically, and morally. The countries more especially under the rule of Aries include Great Britain, Syria, Denmark, lower Poland, Germany, and Palestine. Some of the governed cities include Marseilles, Naples, Florence, Verona, and Cracow.

In horary questions (questions of the hour), the constellation Aries denotes hiding places for thieves, and places not generally known or frequented. It also signifies sandy or hilly ground, a stable for small beasts, recently ploughed lands, and, in houses, the ceiling or plastering.

The flowers of Aries are the amaryllis, signifying unbending pride, and the daisy, denoting chastity or innocence. The gems of Aries are the diamond, signifying chastity again, and the ruby, which denotes a mind free of evil and corrupting thoughts. The colors flavored by this sign are vivid red, bright blue, and yellow.

Well-known personalities born under the influence of this sign include Henry Clay, Bismark, J. P. Morgan, Hans Christian Anderson, Haydn, John Tyler, Raphael, and General Booth of the Salvation Army.

Taurus ♉ (Venus ♀)

The Sign of the Bull

April 20 to May 20

The constellation Taurus, or second house in the heavens, is under the control of the planet Venus. It is a cold, dry, nocturnal, melancholy, fixed, bestial, and southern sign. It

Figure 35

This horary dial is taken from Stowe's Bible Astrology, *privately printed, 1907.*

belongs to the earth triplicity along with Virgo and Capricorn. This sign is generally considered to be an unfortunate one.

Its geographical dominion embraces such countries as Iran, Ireland, Poland, Cyprus, parts of the Soviet Union, parts of China, and Japan. Some of the cities include such places as Dublin, Atlanta, Palermo, Moscow, and Peking.

In horary questions (questions of the hour), the constellation Taurus denotes stables for horses, storage houses on farms, pasture or feeding grounds, cleared land and unplanted fields. In houses, it signifies the cellar, basement, or first floor rooms.

The flowers of Taurus are the hawthorn, representing hope, and the fleur-de-lis, signifying a burning love. The gems of this sign are the emerald, signifying faithfulness, and the moss agate, denoting a long and healthy life. The colors favored by this sign are lemon-yellow and varied shades of blue.

Well-known personalities born under the influence of Taurus include such people as the Duke of Wellington, John Stuart Mill, Hitler, Daniel Defoe, General Ulysses S. Grant, Niccolò Machiavelli, Oliver Cromwell, and Shakespeare.

Gemini II (Mercury ☿)

The Sign of the Twins

May 21 to June 21

Gemini, the third house in the heavens, is a hot, moist, masculine, diurnal, common, double-bodied, sanguine, and humane sign. It belongs to the air triplicity as do Libra and Aquarius. This sign is considered to be barren.

The southwest part of England, the United States, Belgium, lower Egypt, Flanders, and Armenia are within the limits of its geographical rule. Some of the governed cities include Nuremburg, Cordova, London, Versailles, and Brussels.

In horary questions (questions of the hour), the constellation Gemini denotes hills and mountainous areas, silos, barns, closets, and high places. In the home, it signifies walls, halls, and the plaster.

The flowers of Gemini are the wild rose, representing simplicity, and the honeysuckle, denoting generosity and devoted affection. The gems of this sign are the pearl, signifying happiness, and the beryl, denoting everlasting freshness. The colors favored by this sign are orange, scarlet, white, and silver.

Well-known personalities born under the influence of Gemini would include Alexander Pope, Ralph Waldo Emerson, Patrick Henry, Walt Whitman, Peter the Great, and George I of England.

Cancer ♋ (The Moon ☽)

The Sign of the Crab

June 22 to July 21

Cancer, the only house governed by the Moon, is the sign of the summer tropic, particularly fruitful, but extremely cold. It is a watery, moist, feminine, nocturnal, phlegmatic, northerly, movable, weak, and mute sign. It is the first sign of the watery triplicity, and is joined there with Scorpio and Pisces. Cancer is more fruitful than any of the other eleven zodiacal signs. If evil stars are angular to it, there is a great danger of insanity at birth. This constellation was termed by the ancients, unfortunate, but the leading configurations in the horoscope must determine the character of the nativity under its influence.

The geographical dominion of this sign embraces such countries as Africa, Holland, Scotland, New Zealand, and parts of Italy. Some of the two cities falling under its rule are Amsterdam, Venice, Genoa, Milan, Manchester, and New York.

In horary questions (questions of the hour), this constellation signifies the sea, great rivers, lakes and ponds, marshlands, trenches, ditches, and cisterns. It also represents the cellar of a house, a washhouse or laundry room, and the kitchen area.

The flower of Cancer is the water lily, denoting purity of the heart and sweetness of disposition. The gems of this sign are the ruby, signifying forgetfulness in love matters, and the carnelian, denoting leadership. The colors favored by Cancer are green and russet brown.

Well-known personalities born under the influence of Cancer include such names as Mark Twain, John Jacob Astor, Admiral Farragut, Calvin Coolidge, John Quincy Adams, and the Empress Josephine.

Leo ♌ (The Sun ☉)

The Sign of the Lion

July 22 to August 21

The constellation Leo is the only house governed by the Sun, and it is a northern diurnal, fiery, hot, dry, choleric, commanding, and masculine sign. It is also of long ascension, eastern, violent, bestial, and barren. This sign is the middle of the fire triplicity, and is joined there with Aries and Sagittarius. The general disposition of those born under its influence will be resoluteness combined with an unbending temper, yet the latter part of this sign signifies courtesy, and a pleasant manner. Leo is generally esteemed to be a fortunate sign of the zodiac.

The geographical locations subject to its rule are the Alps, Italy, France, Sicily, and western England. Some of the cities under its rule are Rome, Bristol, Bath, Damascus, and Philadelphia.

In horary questions (questions of the hour), this constellation denotes places where wild beasts frequent, including woods,

THE STORY OF THE ZODIAC.

Figure 36

A promotional piece which was used in the late eighteen hundreds by a prominent American astrologer.

forests, deserts, and steep, rocky, inaccessible places. It also signifies palaces, castles, forts, parks, and camping areas. In a house, this sign represents places where fires are kept.

The flower of Leo is the red poppy, signifying consolation. The gems are the sardonyx, denoting marital bliss, the ruby, representing charity and dignity, and the diamond, for purity and joy. The colors favored by Leo are green, red, and orange.

Well-known personalities born under the influence of this sign are Robert Ingersoll, Sarah Kemble Siddons, Napoleon, Lyndon Johnson, Sir Walter Scott, George Bernard Shaw, and Lord Alfred Tennyson.

Virgo ♍ (Mercury ☿)

The Sign of the Virgin

August 22 to September 22

Virgo, the sixth house of the heavens, comprising one half of the zodiac, is the residence of Mercury. This constellation is a melancholy, cold, dry, nocturnal, feminine, southern and barren sign. It is a humane sign of commanding character. Virgo is the middle sign of the earth triplicity, and is accompanied there by Taurus and Capricorn. This constellation is usually considered unfortunate, unless other powerful aspects exist.

The geographical rule of Virgo encompasses such countries as Turkey, Greece, Switzerland, and certain areas in France. Cities under its government are Paris, Jerusalem, and Reading.

In horary questions (questions of the hour), Virgo denotes a study, a library, or any other place where books are kept. It also signifies a closet, a dairy farm, corn fields, grainaries or grain.

The flower of Virgo is the morning glory which signifies peace of mind. The gems are the sapphire, denoting hope, and pink jasper, signifying humility. The colors favored by Virgo are gold, silver, and black or brown.

Well-known personalities born under the influence of this sign include Goethe, James Fenimore Cooper, Oliver Wendell Holmes, and William Henry Harrison.

Libra ♎ (Venus ♀)

The Sign of the Scales

September 23 to October 22

The constellation Libra is the seventh house of the heavens, the abode of Venus, and exaltation of Saturn. It is a hot, moist, airy, sanguine, equinoctial, moving, masculine, cardinal, humane, diurnal, and obeying sign. It belongs to the air triplicity along with Gemini and Aquarius. The ancients held it to be a fortunate sign.

Libra's geographical government extends over Tibet, parts of China and Japan, Austria, Belgium, Portugal, and upper Egypt. Cities falling under its domain are Vienna, Frankfurt, Antwerp, Lisbon, Bombay, and Charleston.

In horary questions (questions of the hour), Libra signifies the sides of hills, where wood is cut, tops of mountains, trees, hunting grounds, sand and gravel fields, pure clean air, an outhouse, or even a barn in need of repair. In a house it represents the upper rooms, a bedroom, the tops of chests and dressers.

The flower of Libra is the hop which denotes a lighthearted attitude and great faith in love matters. The gems are the opal, representing hope and faith, and the diamond, signifying purity. The colors favored by Libra are white, yellow, and crimson.

Well-known personalities born under the influence of this sign include Rutherford B. Hays, Sarah Bernhardt, Franz Liszt, Dwight D. Eisenhower, and Lord Nelson.

Scorpio ♏ (Mars ♂)

The Sign of the Scorpion

October 23 to November 21

Scorpio, one of the most evil and unfortunate of the zodiac signs, is in the eighth house of the heavens, and the abode of Mars. It is a cold, watery, phlegmatic, northern, nocturnal, feminine, moist, fixed, fruitful sign of long ascension. Deceit, fraud, and hypocrisy are its peculiar and general characteristics. It is the middle sign of the water triplicity and is accompanied there by Cancer and Pisces. The ancients accounted Scorpio, as they well might, unfortunate.

It rules, geographically, Norway, upper Bavaria, Morocco, Algiers, and parts of England. Cities falling under its government include Liverpool, Oslo, and Ghent.

In horary questions (questions of the hour), Scorpio represents all types of creeping insects that are known to be poisonous and found in gardens, orchards, stagnant lakes, ponds, muddy grounds, and kitchens. It also denotes the above areas as well as the bugs.

The flower of Scorpio is the chrysanthemum, signifying truth. The gems are the topaz, denoting honesty in love, and the malachite, representing close attachment. The colors favored by Scorpio are various shades of brown, dark blue, and black.

Well-known personalities born under the influence of this sign include Richard the Third, Marie Antoinette, Martin Luther, Robert Louis Stevenson, Sir William Herschel, and John Adams.

𝔖agittarius ♐ (𝔍upiter ♃)

The Sign of the Archer

November 22 to December 21

The constellation Sagittarius, in the ninth house of the heavens, is the joy and abode of Jupiter. It is a fiery, masculine, dry, diurnal, changeable, southern, fruitful, choleric, common, and bicorporal or double-bodied sign. It is the third or negative part of the fire triplicity, and is accompanied there by Aries and Leo. Sagittarius was deemed a fortunate sign by the ancients.

This constellation geographically rules over such nations as Hungary, Spain, Dalmatia, and Moravia. Cities falling under its domain include Cologne, Madrid, Budapest, and Sheffield.

In horary questions (questions of the hour), Sagittarius denotes horse stables, or a barn where four-footed animals are boarded, a field, hills, and high points of land or grounds that rise a little above the rest. It signifies the upper rooms of houses and places near a fireplace or a stove.

The flower of Sagittarius is the holly, symbolizing foresight. The gems are the turquoise, signifying prosperity, and the carbuncle, denoting friendship and true love. The colors favored by Sagittarius are green, red, and gold.

Well-known personalities born under the influence of this sign include Ignace Paderewski, John Milton, Martin Van Buren, George VI of England, Jonathan Swift, and President Franklin Pierce.

ℭapricornus ♑ (𝔖aturn ♄)

The Sign of the Goat

December 22 to January 20

Capricorn (the horned goat), is in the tenth house of the heavens, and is the abode of Saturn and the exaltation of Mars.

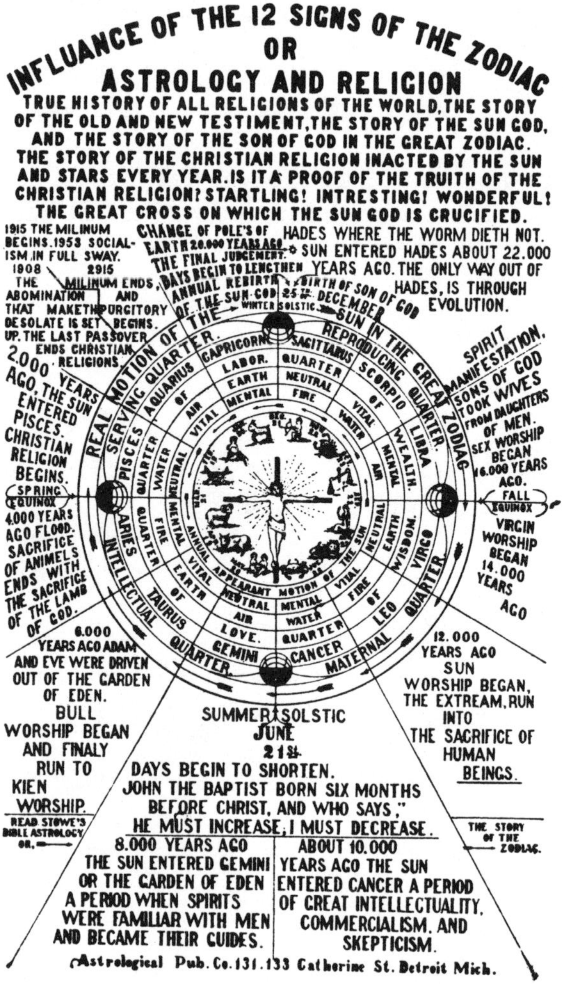

Figure 37

An advertisement which appeared throughout the United States in the late eighteen hundreds.

It is cold, earthy, sterile, nocturnal, obeying, movable, changeable, melancholy, cardinal, feminine, and southern sign. It is the last part of the earth triplicity that includes Taurus and Virgo. Its legitimate possessor is said to be the most evil and malignant of all the planets. In nativities, it is the most destructive. There is no planetary aspect, however powerful, that can avert its influence. The ancients classed Capricorn among the unfortunate signs.

The geographical divisions of earth under the power of this constellation include India, Bulgaria, Albania, Mexico, and Greece. Cities ruled are Oxford, Bombay, Bradenburg, and Mexico City.

In horary questions (questions of the hour), this sign denotes barns, tool sheds, animal pens, barren fields, thorny bushes, and dark places near the ground.

The flower of Capricorn is the snowdrop, a symbol of hope and consolation. The gems of this sign are the garnet, denoting true and lasting friendship, and the moonstone, signifying thoughtful friendship. The colors favored by Capricorn are garnet and silver.

Well-known personalities born under the influence of this sign include Edgar Allen Poe, Daniel Webster, Robert E. Lee, Disraeli, Gladstone, and Alexander Hamilton.

Aquarius ♒ (Saturn ♄)

The Sign of the Water-Bearer

January 21 to February 19

Aquarius, the dwelling place of Saturn, and the eleventh house of the heavens, is a sanguine, aerial, hot, moist, masculine, obeying sign. It is also western, diurnal, fixed, and humane. Aquarius is the third part of the air triplicity and is accompanied there by Gemini and Libra. It is deemed a fortunate sign.

It holds geographic sway over such places as the Soviet Union, Sweden, Denmark, and parts of Germany. Cities falling under its influence include Hamburg, Copenhagen, Bremen, and Stockholm.

In horary questions (questions of the hour), this sign represents hilly places, uneven fields, newly dug or ploughed areas, quarries, vineyards, or little springs. In houses, this sign denotes the roof, eaves, or upper parts.

The flower of Aquarius is the primrose, a symbol of early youth and simplicity. The gems of this sign are the amethyst, denoting sincerity, true love, and faith, and the sapphire, signifying faith and lasting friendship. The colors favored by Aquarius are pink, nile-green, and yellow.

Well-known personalities born under the influence of this sign include Mozart, Mendelssohn, Robert Burns, Byron, George Washington, Abraham Lincoln, Charles Dickens, Darwin, Francis Bacon, Franklin Delano Roosevelt, Charles Lindberg, and Voltaire.

Pisces ♓ (Jupiter ♃)

The Sign of the Fish

February 20 to March 20

Pisces (the fishes), the twelfth and last among the signs of the zodiac in the houses of heaven, is the abode of Jupiter and the exaltation of Venus. It is a moist, cold, watery, effeminate, nocturnal, southern, obeying, phlegmatic, common, bicorporeal, sickly sign representing a person of no action. It is the last of the water triplicity and is accompanied there by Cancer and Scorpio. It is a fruitful and luxuriant sign—but is deemed unfortunate.

Pisces rules such geographic areas as Portugal, parts of Spain, Normandy, Alexandria, and Worms.

In horary questions (questions of the hour), it represents grounds full of water, or places where there are many springs and many fowl. It also includes ponds and rivers full of fish and houses near water.

The flower of Pisces is the violet, a sign of great modesty. The gems of this sign are the bloodstone, symbolizing courage, and the chrysolite, denoting protection against madness, covetousness, and foolish actions. The colors favored by this sign are pure white, emerald green, and all light shades.

Well-known personalities born under the influence of this sign include Jean Meissonier, Victor Hugo, Copernicus, Frederic Chopin, Rachel, Van Dyck, Grover Cleveland, Rossini, Handel, Michelangelo, and James Madison.

BOOK XIX
the mystical oracle
of destiny

This ancient Oracle of Destiny contains a series of twenty-six questions, listed from A to Z. Each of these individual questions can be answered accurately by following the directions as given. The Wheel of Destiny must be consulted initially. You will note that this mystic wheel contains every letter of the alphabet, each one within a square. Under each letter is a number.

Take the numbers allocated to the first letters of each of your names. Then write down the day of the month on which you were born. Now refer to the table with gives the mystic numbers of the days and the planets. If you happen to be asking your question on a Wednesday, take the number that is placed under this particular day on the table, as well as the number given for that planet. Total all of these numbers together, and carefully divide by twenty. The remainder will be your *key* number, the one which will unlock the secrets of the Mystic Number Table.

For example, suppose a person named Beverly Jo Jensen were to consult this oracle, and ask question "E," *Will the person who is sick recover, or will he have a relapse?* She asks this question on a Tuesday, and she was born on the fourteenth of the month. This information would be calculated as follows:

6 = number for (B) Beverly, Wheel of Destiny.
11 = number for (J) Jo, Wheel of Destiny.
11 = number for (J) Jensen, Wheel of Destiny.

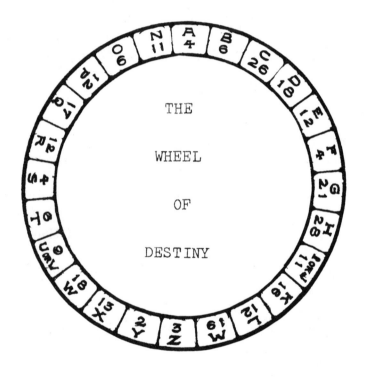

Figure 38

This illustration of the Wheel of Destiny appeared in an old 1670 manuscript.

14 = day of the month she was born.

78 = number for Tuesday, the day the question was asked, from the table of Day and Planet numbers.

48 = number for Mars, from the table of Day and Planet numbers.

———

168 = Total

Now the total of 168 is divided by twenty (20), and a remainder of eight (8) is left over, your *key* to the Mystic Number Table. Turn to this special table on pages 178-179 and find the number eight (8) in the top row of figures. Follow this column down until you come to the line of the fifth question, "E," the one you asked. You will see that these two lines intersect at the number twelve (12) on the table. This new number tells you which is the correct section to look under in the Table of Mystic Answers. Then, turn to section 12 in the answers, and locate the letter "E," which corresponds with the letter in the original question. This will give you the correct answer. In this particular case, it will read: *A new doctor is required. Recovery will be delayed.*

Twenty-Six Mystic Questions

A. Will I experience good or bad fortune now or later?

B. When will I become wealthy, if at all?

C. Shall I obtain everything I desire?

D. What are the initials of the person I should see?

E. Will the person who is sick recover, or will he have a relapse?

Mystic Planet and Mystic Day Numbers

Saturday	Sunday	Monday	Tuesday
48	103	61	78
Saturn	Sun	Moon	Mars
50	39	41	48

Mystic Number Table

	1	2	3	4	5	6	7	8	9	10	11	12	13
Question													
A	1	2	3	4	5	6	7	8	9	10	11	12	13
B	2	3	4	5	6	7	8	9	10	11	12	13	14
C	3	4	5	6	7	8	9	10	11	12	13	14	15
D	4	5	6	7	8	9	10	11	12	13	14	15	16
E	5	6	7	8	9	10	11	12	13	14	15	16	17
F	6	7	8	9	10	11	12	13	14	15	16	17	18
G	7	8	9	10	11	12	13	14	15	16	17	18	19
H	8	9	10	11	12	13	14	15	16	17	18	19	20
I	9	10	11	12	13	14	15	16	17	18	19	20	21
J	10	11	12	13	14	15	16	17	18	19	20	21	22
K	11	12	13	14	15	16	17	18	19	20	21	22	23
L	12	13	14	15	16	17	18	19	20	21	22	23	24
M	13	14	15	16	17	18	19	20	21	22	23	24	25
N	14	15	16	17	18	19	20	21	22	23	24	25	26
O	15	16	17	18	19	20	21	22	23	24	25	26	1
P	16	17	18	19	20	21	22	23	24	25	26	1	2
Q	17	18	19	20	21	22	23	24	25	26	1	2	3
R	18	19	20	21	22	23	24	25	26	1	2	3	4
S	19	20	21	22	23	24	25	26	1	2	3	4	5
T	20	21	22	23	24	25	26	1	2	3	4	5	6
U	21	22	23	24	25	26	1	2	3	4	5	6	7
V	22	23	24	25	26	1	2	3	4	5	6	7	8
W	23	24	25	26	1	2	3	4	5	6	7	8	9
X	24	25	26	1	2	3	4	5	6	7	8	9	10
Y	25	26	1	2	3	4	5	6	7	8	9	10	11
Z	26	1	2	3	4	5	6	7	8	9	10	11	12

Mystic Planet and Mystic Day Numbers (Continued)

Wednesday	Thursday	Friday
109	37	89
Mercury	Jupiter	Venus
119	83	53

Mystic Number Table

	14	15	16	17	18	19	20	21	22	23	24	25	26
Questions													
A	14	15	16	17	18	19	20	21	22	23	24	25	26
B	15	16	17	18	19	20	21	22	23	24	25	26	1
C	16	17	18	19	20	21	22	23	24	25	26	1	2
D	17	18	19	20	21	22	23	24	25	26	1	2	3
E	18	19	20	21	22	23	24	25	26	1	2	3	4
F	19	20	21	22	23	24	25	26	1	2	3	4	5
G	20	21	22	23	24	25	26	1	2	3	4	5	6
H	21	22	23	24	25	26	1	2	3	4	5	6	7
I	22	23	24	25	26	1	2	3	4	5	6	7	8
J	23	24	25	26	1	2	3	4	5	6	7	8	9
K	24	25	26	1	2	3	4	5	6	7	8	9	10
L	25	26	1	2	3	4	5	6	7	8	9	10	11
M	26	1	2	3	4	5	6	7	8	9	10	11	12
N	1	2	3	4	5	6	7	8	9	10	11	12	13
O	2	3	4	5	6	7	8	9	10	11	12	13	14
P	3	4	5	6	7	8	9	10	11	12	13	14	15
Q	4	5	6	7	8	9	10	11	12	13	14	15	16
R	5	6	7	8	9	10	11	12	13	14	15	16	17
S	6	7	8	9	10	11	12	13	14	15	16	17	18
T	7	8	9	10	11	12	13	14	15	16	17	18	19
U	8	9	10	11	12	13	14	15	16	17	18	19	20
V	9	10	11	12	13	14	15	16	17	18	19	20	21
W	10	11	12	13	14	15	16	17	18	19	20	21	22
X	11	12	13	14	15	16	17	18	19	20	21	22	23
Y	12	13	14	15	16	17	18	19	20	21	22	23	24
Z	13	14	15	16	17	18	19	20	21	22	23	24	25

F. Will I live a long life or will I die relatively young?

G. What is my ultimate destiny? My planetary sign?

H. Is my friend honest and faithful?

I. How will the weather turn out for that special occasion?

J. What is to be my fate concerning marriage?

K. What is to be my friend's fate concerning marriage?

L. Will I win or lose in a law suit?

M. Will I win or lose if I attempt to gamble?

N. Shall I take a trip at this time?

O. Where should I go on this trip?

P. I am thinking of a particular day. Will it prove fortunate?

Q. What is the most important day of the week or month for me?

R. Do I have more friends or enemies?

S. What can you inform me as to stolen things?

T. What is in store for the next seven years?

U. What type of business will prosper for me?

V. Must I relocate in order to succeed?

W. Will there be a change in my life this coming year?

X. Will my present bad fortune change for the better?

Y. Will my newest speculations prove successful?·

Z. Who is to be the victor in the soon to come fight?

Table of Mystic Answers

Table One

A. Bad luck reigns from 20 to 25; better fortune from 27 to 30; evil from 31 to 39; good fortune thereafter.

B. Manifold omens deny any great accumulation of wealth.

C. Why seek financial riches? The stars allot you many good years of fortune.

D. An admirer's name, often spoken within your hearing, begins with a G; someone who is a thief, with an F.

E. The signs appear to flatter those who are ill, but there is some doubt noted, and possible coming danger.

F. This omen designates perils by poison and possible accidents. There is a danger period during the thirty-second year of life.

G. Venus rules. Your fate is to do much traveling abroad, then returning in prosperity. You will see many dignitaries.

H. Several of the stars speak favorably. You will find both qualities in love and friendship. There is something foreshadowed that indicates great prosperity in the near future.

I. It will be cloudy and possibly raining in the winter; in the spring, hail and thunder; in the summer, fine weather, but stormy at intervals; in the autumn, thunder.

J. You are destined to wed a prudent, sensible person, who has a fair complexion and gray eyes; one born near you, met through a mutual friend. Wealthy relatives will condemn and despise the both of you. Take care to rile none of these people.

K. To marry one both short and rather ugly, from a distant land, who is extremely fortunate.

L. You have a minimum of three opponents in the case. One you do not expect. Some delays will upset you, but stay cheerful.

M. Evil omens are all around you. Escape while you still can. Be cautious. Someone is planning to lure you into serious losses through cheating.

N. There is danger brewing. All signs are contrary to you in this respect. Be most careful for peril accompanies any trip by air or water, and a sudden alarm if traveling by land.

O. South by land; west by air. You should restrain all traveling for seven seasons—one year and nine months.

P. The planetary signs are all on your side. The omens all flatter you. If you are thinking in terms of love, you will succeed in a wonderfully unexpected manner.

Q. Thursday is the most important day. Sunday your unfortunate day. Wednesday your luckiest. The third day of the moon will be one to remember after you reach twenty-three.

R. This sign tells of three friends, all tall and dark, one a female. A secret enemy is at present plotting against you.

S. Anything lost is gone for good. You will never recover these items. Stolen things will be heard of and possibly recovered.

T. The mysterious stars assuredly speak of better fortune for you. Be joyful and gay. All things will work out well in three years. This next year will start with improvements.

U. None. Seek instead some other type of enterprise. Church work, property investment, and dreary mansions hold some gain.

V. You had better consider this seriously before taking any action in haste. There will assuredly be changes if you stay.

W. A narrow escape from death; a funeral; a false friend; a series of fortunate events for six months.

X. In only seven days your fortune will change for the better, and something will happen materially to affect your dreams.

Y. If it's financial speculation you ask about, it will. If of love and marriage, or sensuous pleasures of any kind, it is dubious.

Z. The taller of the two will overcome all adversity. There are definite signs of frustration which may change the matter.

Table Two

A. Fortune will favor you with her choicest boons during the cycle of middle age. Beware of your thirty-third year, and also of your forty-second. Evil planetary signs proclaim these years as potentially disastrous.

B. If you have not asked for an impossibility; it will take place. There are, at present, and will continue to be, some minor difficulties in the path.

C. Your desires are simply too much to hope for. Do not trust the stars for they flatter at this time.

D. The principal name of a lover begins with an E; a thief's name with a C, and it is short.

E. This person is, at present, in serious jeopardy, but is destined to escape. The first and seventh days from today are critical, but the twentieth day will show improvement.

F. Several accidents will befall you. One will be by fire, another by horse, and the third by a dog. Twice more you will be periled by men you do not know at present.

G. The Sun is your planetary genius, and foretells many ambitious exploits. Try always to excel.

H. Your friend is now happy. All goes well so do not worry.

I. Do you ask about today or tomorrow? If so then rain is in the air. If in the future, expect thunder in the summer, gales in the spring, and hail in the fall.

J. You will love a great many, deceive most of them, and will eventually meet more than your match in marriage.

K. He or she will marry twice. One choice will be light, someone who is yet a stranger. The other will be dark, and elderly. The second marriage will certainly be the happiest.

L. However bad it seems now to be, your stars speak in favor of your excellent good fortune. Worry not.

M. Be on guard and bet with extreme care. One opponent will be treacherous. Some of your signs denote mischief.

N. Success will be at your side if you initiate a trip only while the moon is increasing, at least seven days before it is full, and on a Monday. However, expect alarms while traveling.

O. Shun any water. Travel only to the northern part of the state or country in which you reside at present, at least this year.

P. Harm is near at hand. Postpone any plans for the day you are thinking about for at least three months.

Q. Wednesday is the most pernicious day of your life. The eighth day of every month is your most fortunate.

R. You cast an omen of rancor, and are surrounded with a number of adversaries. Remember to have caution against malice.

S. You will never recover the stolen goods, but the thief will be caught within the year and justice will triumph.

T. You will mourn three times; have trouble with a female friend; make an unexpected journey; make a powerful enemy; and be given a very expensive gift. You may possibly suffer a wound.

U. Success is promised in business dealing with books, music, or pictures. Do not try banking or speculating.

V. A well-contemplated change of scenery would help, but do not leave for at least four weeks and two days for fear of evil.

W. You are destined to suffer greatly for the year to come. Then the evil influence will leave your life.

X. The planet Venus tells of a birth. The good fortune you ask for will follow soon after.

Y. Three perils will have to be faced squarely or you will lose. You will come close to giving up the project. Success is doubtful for at least another year.

Z. Both shall lose, and this will annoy you to no end.

Table Three

A. Between the ages of fourteen and twenty-five your life is fair in prospects, yet subject to some evils. Between thirty-five and forty-two, expect exceedingly good fortune.

B. The star of your destiny is obscured at present. Your fate is crossed for at least three months. Ask again at that time.

C. The planetary signs are indeed fortunate, but one person will work against you. Beware of an enemy hiding behind friendship.

D. The name you seek is a long one with many syllables. It begins with an I or a J. You know this individual rather well.

E. There are signs of a mysterious relapse. By all means, change physicians and avoid this danger. Keep the sickroom free of drafts except for air from open window tops.

F. There is much trouble ahead in your life. Much has passed, and more is yet to come. Your middle age, from thirty-nine to fifty-five, is the most generous. After sixty will be even better.

G. Mercury is looking after your interests. Your destiny is to become well known and famous in your day and generation.

H. Great deceit is manifest in the friend of whom you inquire. Be exceedingly watchful and practice prudence in all matters.

I. It will be wet and snowy if in the winter, and cloudy and wet if in the spring or summer.

J. To marry someone you love mildly, yet prize highly. You will do well in this union. It brings bountiful fortune.

K. Three suitors will court this individual. The darkest, with eyes of hazel, will be selected for marriage.

L. The verdict will be against you, but no money will change hands. You will be most fortunate in this case.

M. If you win now, you will suffer great losses later.

N. You will travel safely only if the trip is begun while the moon is in the sign of Capricorn, the goat.

O. Do not travel far from the place of your birth. Avoid going southward. The stars indicate evils and perplexities.

P. Slander and other ill reports are foretold by the stars. Be on guard that nothing unworthy is pursued on that day.

Q. Thursday is your best day for good fortune. Saturday for evil tidings. The fifteenth day of every month will be notable.

R. There will be a multitude of enemies, but few friends.

S. Stolen goods will sometimes be recovered in part. Things lost will never be found so don't bother looking.

T. The bearings of the planets foretell a wedding; a long and perilous trip; and numerous changes. Fortune is fickle.

U. Wealth will come slowly, but trouble quickly, in any type of business enterprise. Never lend either money or your name.

V. You should not move for at least a year and six months.

W. Manifold crosses are evident. Take heed of this omen.

X. There will soon be a drastic change for the better.

Y. Whatever you intend, examine it once more before going ahead with it. Use what measures you can to insure success.

Z. The dark-haired person will be the visitor.

Table Four

A. Fortune will favor you after twenty-nine years of age, and your old age certainly will not be spent in poverty.

B. The stars presage prosperity, but you must be patient.

C. All of your signs indicate good fortune.

D. R is the letter concerning love; any other person, W.

E. A quick recovery is near at hand.

F. It is possible you may, if you are more prudent.

G. The Sun and Mercury rule. You will roam restlessly. You are fortune's favorite at times, her football at others.

H. Be careful in whom you confide. You will do well to remember the caution given here.

I. If you ask about a particular day, it will be dry and pleasant. If about a season, the reverse.

J. You will marry young, and follow your mate to the grave. Your second mate will bring you wealth, but little happiness.

K. Three times in love, but never will the love be returned. Yet, you will ultimately marry quite well.

L. By the exertion of much diligence you will finally win.

M. You may win, but take care thereafter. Those who play these games of chance rarely are winners in the end.

N. There will be serious dangers and possibly a rival.

O. East, avoiding the air in all cases.

P. Yes, but it is better always to shun a Friday.

Q. Thursday is your best day. Friday, the most notable. Sunday the day of evil fortune for you, as well as the first day of the new moon.

R. The signs are portentous of enemies and adversaries.

S. Stolen articles will be recovered, while lost items will not be found for a period of two weeks if at all.

T. Three relatives are to die; unexpected circumstances will elevate you in stature; four changes, three for evil, one for good.

U. By the simple extension of natural talent will you succeed best. A traveling-type career, supplying the needs of the rich.

V. It is best to plan on this within two months.

W. It will drastically change in three months, and in three years, three changes for the better will take place.

X. Your fortune for the past two years has been fickle, but a friend who will help you is soon to return.

Y. The planetary signs indicate a troublesome time for one week. After this period, it will change. The good planets shine.

Z. The darker of the two combatants will be the winner.

Table Five

A. Between the ages of thirty-one and forty-nine, and during the extreme of life will be your best times.

B. The planets lean toward good fortune in this matter.

C. If your desire is regarding business, yes; love, no.

D. N, if you seek a name in love matters; S begins an uncouth name; W is the first letter of a thief's name.

E. Doubt is foretold by the stars. There is danger to come, but recovery is certain. Someone in the home of the ill disagrees.

F. There is one malady implied in three years, but you will overcome this and be long-lived.

G. Venus and Mercury rule your fate. You are destined to a marvelous fortune of notability and wealth. Some calamities.

H. That he presently is, cannot be doubted, but the stars will not vouch that he will remain so over four months.

I. If in the summer, expect unhealthy weather. If you ask about one particular day, it will be opposed to your desires.

J. You will find it extremely difficult, unbelievably so, to meet with much true happiness in wedlock.

K. Hymen's yoke will press heavily, but contentment will surely bring forth happiness in the end.

L. If you hearken to the advice of the stars and follow the wishes of the wise, you will ultimately gain greatly.

M. The signs presage that you will win.

N. To travel at this time, or for the coming year, will bring ill-luck.

O. You will gain in love by going west, and a wife may be yours. There is grave misfortune if you go south.

P. This is to be doubted for the stars are unclear in this regard. You can never be certain.

Q. The fifth and fifteenth day of each month may bring sorrow or anxiety. Monday will be the most remarkable day of your life.

R. You have many more friends, but not long ago it was the reverse.

S. Look for lost items in closets. The chances of recovering stolen things runs two to one against you.

T. A marriage, a birth, great losses, a reversal, fear of a loss by fire and thievery, and a relocation. Also a feast, burial, and great prejudice by some woman.

U. Try this oracle another time. The stars now deny you.

V. The stars in heaven speak affirmatively in this matter.

W. There will be changes in destiny, fate, and fortune and, moreover, you are to be unsettled for at least eight months.

X. Hard work, sorrow, and unrest are presently foreshadowed. Six months will bring changes for the better.

Y. A remarkably singular thing is even now happening.

Z. The aspects of the planets, as they now tend to look, are rather uncertain. The tallest is most likely to be victorious.

Table Six

A. The fifth seven years, counting from the day of birth, are the best in fortune. After this the stars are cloudy.

B. The stars do not speak favorably of finances, but they are extremely good regarding friends, love matters, and pleasure.

C. Do not be misled by foolish joy, nor cast down by despair. The hope will, in part, be fulfilled, but were all dreams fulfilled, you would be far from satisfied.

D. If you ask of a lover, V; M, if of a thief. Both names will seem strange to you, one seldom spoken.

E. The planets promise health, although things look bad now.

F. There are many struggles to overcome, but you are destined to outlive your contemporaries and relations.

G. The Sun smiles down upon you and foretells a long life, a great name, wealth, and happiness. But four times in earlier years you will be periled by a singular danger.

H. Expect the worst. Infinite trouble and ill-luck are seen.

I. Clear and sunny if you seek a day or a week. If a special month or more, the signs are doubtful.

J. Your choice of a mate is worthy of great respect and faithfulness. You are more fortunate than most.

K. To meet an admirer who will be a tormenter, but later to happily marry richly. Happiness is in store.

L. A bribe or some treachery is portended. There is doubt that your side of the cause will be conducted well.

M. Be cautious how and what you bet. Deceivers will be close at hand. Do not forget this warning.

N. Do not travel by foot or automobile at this time.

O. Go east during the summer months or not at all.

P. It is most likely that it will.

Q. Monday is the most remarkable day for you. You will wed on that particular day, or something of infinite importance will surely happen. Tuesday is always one of sad recollections.

R. The planets foretell annoyance where friendship should be expected. Beware of hypocrisy and pretending friends.

S. A diligent search will recover lost or stolen things.

T. An irregular train of events: some will be flattering, some the reverse. Scandal will hurt. Many gifts and crosses.

U. The investment of other people's money and bartering.

V. Extraordinary precautions will be necessary. The planets bear the expression of evil.

W. Science will open new paths for the industrious. Persevere and your life will be strewn with roses.

X. The planets foreshadow numerous progeny, and fortune goes well before them. Take heed of this omen.

Y. Be thankful that the planets are so fortunate with you.

Z. A bloodless fight with few blows will result in an exchange of money. This will overcome all anger.

Table Seven

A. Fickle stars proclaim the fear of great evil and annoyance.

B. Money is to be yours wherever you go throughout the world.

C. The stars indicate evil at this moment. Seek your answer at another time. Try the oracle in one week from today.

D. If you ask in relation to wedlock or love, the initial is K or J. If about a thief, an R.

E. The stars are threatening and the omen is one of evil.

F. Long life is not promised, but life well spent, is.

G. The Sun again rules here and predicts great esteem among friends and kindred. Few will reach the pinnacle of your fate.

H. Expect the worst, but hope for the best.

I. The summer season will turn out to be wet and windy, but if you ask of a particular day it will be stormy, especially if the moon is past full. Postpone your plans.

J. To wed someone with a great deal of money, but to have a serious number of domestic broils and discords.

K. A prudent mate is your lot, after trouble of getting them has passed. Look well to your intentions.

L. Beware of unexpected deceitfulness. There is something afoot between those who advise you in the legal matter.

M. The stars and the planets deny winning—they threaten enormous losses. Better not to gamble at all now.

N. There are omens of evil in traveling by water, but if by land, you will be safe.

O. Due south, but avoid the northeast at all costs. It will be imprudent to travel extensively for at least one year.

P. If you consult this oracle in earnest, you shall gain all wishes for that special day.

Q. Saturday will be that day. Also look to the tenth day of each month as important and eventful in your life.

R. There is a sign of one bitter enemy. Beware of deceit.

S. Stolen things are too far away for recovery. Look in a drawer for things you have lost.

T. Much illness and possible disease; three funerals; seven major changes; an unexpected adventure; and a birth.

U. Publishing, manufacturing, and selling medicines, and selling books and other paper merchandise.

V. You must use your own judgment at this time for the planets signify wiles and deceit.

W. A change is due in twenty-seven days.

X. Your inquiry is in vain, or at the least, fickle and insincere. Try once more, in an hour from this time.

Y. There is no sign of evil import and, even if there were, a friendly star protects you in all ways.

Z. You will finally overcome all enemies although a world of difficulties is foreshadowed. Be extremely prudent.

Table Eight

A. The morning of your life will be blissful; a somber cloud appears in your twenties; and your middle age from thirty-nine on will be the most fruitful. There is a rainbow of hope.

B. All is not gold that seems to glitter. Do not expect too much from life. The stars are not wholly in your favor.

C. The planets denote a variety of good things starting on the fourth day from this. Twenty-six days will decide your fate.

D. The unknown party has a quaint old name starting with E.

E. The fourth week will decide this matter. It will seem very dangerous for the next three days.

F. There are signs of weakness visible, but your planet seems to indicate a relatively long life.

G. Saturn rules. You will have a diversified life, enriched by the labors of many others.

H. The friend whom you ask about is as you wish. This does not refer to the future. Be careful a year from today.

I. If a certain day, it will turn out contrary to your wishes.

J. You will marry a discreet person, one you love deeply. Less freedom than you now have will be a point of argument.

K. To marry someone who is at present a complete stranger. Your fortune is subject to many annoying changes due to this.

L. You cannot be overly cautious because false witnesses will rise up against you. You may be foiled in the end.

M. You will, at first, lose a trifle, but if cheating is not practiced, you will surely win.

N. Consult this oracle again before setting out, and begin only on a fortunate day. Travel by land.

O. Travel anywhere, but avoid mountain country if you wish to succeed. You will gain most by going westward.

P. The stars near you are harmonious and good. Fortune in great measure is in your favor.

Q. Saturday is the day you will most repent in your life. Tuesday is the day on which you must be careful. The twenty-seventh of October will prove to be the brightest day each year.

R. You will have mostly enemies but fortune does smile. A full share of happiness will be yours.

S. Part will be recovered. Look for lost things in a bedroom.

T. A total change in your business pursuits, four accidents, and minor bruises. One of the next seven years will be the most fortunate of your life. Take advantage of this time.

U. You will gain from the rich, but will lose in trading.

V. Relocate within eight days. It will be a lucky move.

W. This foretells many happy successes.

X. Doubtlessly it will. This is the forerunner of wealth, prosperity, love, and happiness.

Y. The next two hours are evil, and evil-minded persons will try to vex you. Try again tomorrow.

Z. The tallest of the two will overcome the other, either personally or by proxy. The weaker of the two will afterwards become close friends with the conquerer.

Table Nine

A. Some calamities and disasters, with three narrow escapes, during the next three years of fickle fortune. Then prosperity will finally arrive. Be patient.

B. You seek that of which you must not ask further particulars for at least three more months. No answer is forthcoming.

C. Your fate is foreshadowed to be evil at twenty-one, and perilous at twenty-nine. Temperance and fortitude will aid you.

D. Do you inquire of a lover? If so then the name starts with an O. If an enemy or thief, N or P.

E. Two crisis have passed recently. Cherish hope, for the stars foreshadow only good from this point on.

F. There is a spell of illness coming. Until this has passed, the planets will not foretell the length of your life.

G. The Sun rules over you. It bodes good luck and success.

H. They are sick and in trouble. Be not uneasy with them.

I. If you ask about a particular month, it will be pleasant. If asking of a special day, it will be dry and beautiful.

J. You are destined to marry a prudent and clever person. It will be a stranger from the east, one whom you love very much.

K. A slow and tiresome courtship, but then a quick marriage. It will be a fortunate marriage for all concerned.

L. If you are able to keep false witnesses away, then fear not. Your enemy will be powerful and wealthy.

M. Fortune is yours. What more would you have?

N. Mark this well! By land there is safety. Do not peril yourself on water. Avoid travel while the moon is full.

O. Travel westward away from your birthplace or from where you presently are. Otherwise do not go at all. Never go east.

P. Fate is opposed to your wishes. This sign speaks of a secret snare, one designed to mislead you.

Q. Monday is your greatest day for success. Friday will prove to be the most sorrowful day of your life.

R. Your friends preponderate. Six favor you, four against.

S. A woman is deeply involved in this theft.

T. Within three months you will perceive the change that will influence your entire future. In three years an even greater one.

U. The aqueous signs influence this part of your life. If you are to prosper, choose something related to the sea.

V. If you move at present it will only increase the evils around you. Beware of changing under five months and a day.

W. You will relocate suddenly and quite unexpectedly where there will be plenty of employment. A friend will assist you.

X. Beware of a red-headed person. The planets warn against deceit, cunning, and hatred so be always on guard.

Y. Propitious signs abound around you. Be cautious, for one sign indicates a few months' delay, and a possible setback.

Z. Some delay will be caused, but you are destined to be the victor after a short perilous period of time.

Table Ten

A. Your youth is fraught with many vicissitudes. Success will come only after much patience and struggling.

B. You will enjoy the luxuries of wealth, and this is to commence one year from this day. Be prudent or it will be lost.

C. Take heed that you are not overly ardent in your wishes. There is a serious possibility that you will not gain everything.

D. The name of one who is enamoured by your charm has a name starting with S. In any other name it is M.

E. The disease is undergoing a change as you ask this. In three days, a crisis. The result will be known then.

F. There are at least three danger periods that could cut your life short. Live more carefully and be prudent.

G. Venus is your planet. You will rise above present expectations, have a pompous name, and gifts of wealth.

H. The friend may be relied on as true.

I. The day will be wet and raining. If it is a season you ask about, it will be rather tempestuous.

J. You will woo and marry someone from a distant land.

K. To marry one bred with money and material goods. A rover by profession, fair-haired, and nice appearing.

L. Mars signifies deceit about you. It will be doubtful for another three months and this will end for you.

M. You will often be a winner. Fortune is surely on your side if you are sincere when consulting the oracle. Play boldly.

N. Go not by air for slow and tedious omens proclaim evil.

O. To low and watery areas. Try a city or small island.

P. The right road to fortune is before you. The stars proclaim one enemy in the path of success. The day is wonderful.

Q. The third day of every month is evil for you. Sunday is always fortunate, and will be the most notable day in your life.

R. Few worldly friendships, yet good is close at hand.

S. One under seventeen has committed the theft. If anything has been misplaced, search in high places where books are kept.

T. The planets indicate a destiny of changeable fate.

U. You will become rich by dealing in merchandise or farming.

V. The planets are presently obscured. Try this again in an hour, or before leaving the house.

W. Who shall doubt the message of the stars? The planets foretell of successful and happy changes.

X. This signifies safety, and of news within ten days.

Y. Your fortune is extremely fickle. An opponent will vex you. By all means, revise your present investment methods.

Z. The fairer of the two will lose in combat. One is backed by friends of stature and position. The end will be curious.

Table Eleven

A. You may expect but very little good luck up until your thirty-second year. Thereafter things will be extremely good.

B. The omens speak of poverty near at hand, and then of a sudden elevation in fortune. Be patient for it will come.

C. After some strife you may. The omens are not decisive, therefore, do not hope for too much.

D. The initial of your future marriage partner is T. If concerning a friend, N, and a thief, W.

E. There will be an important change for the better in four short days. But if the sick person is not careful, there will surely be another relapse, this time maybe disastrous.

F. It would be best not to inquire further into this matter. Perils must be withstood before you reach forty.

G. Venus is allotted to you in your fate. The stars foretell a life full of changes, some good and many bad.

H. Some of the planets are opposed, some decidedly evil. At any rate, be on guard while the moon is near full.

I. The weather will be exceptionally good.

J. You will be disappointed in your first love, and will mourn for three sad years over this apparently evil fate.

K. A host of admirers will be rejected before one is selected who will cherish and worship the feet of the loved one.

L. Why do you ask? The stars predict many bitter enemies. Your personal star will carry you to victory in the final analysis.

M. If you ask this question while expecting to gain, then in this instance you shall lose tremendous sums.

N. Six tedious journeys are allotted you, three by air. Two will be to attend funerals.

O. You are generally unlucky in traveling, but if you must do this, go southward, and stay near dry land.

P. Although a number of the planets presage the day as evil, you can avoid much of it by being discreet and cautious.

Q. Sunday will be your one most remarkable day. The seventeenth of October and the thirteenth of August are days of bad fortune.

R. You have many more friends than enemies at the present time. It will reverse itself in one year. Fortune is yours for at least this year. Utilize it wisely to your benefit.

S. If something is stolen it will not be recovered for it has been taken far away over water. If mislaid, look in a closet.

T. The portents of the next seven years speak only of good.

U. Seek employment in governmental work for there you will succeed without much effort, and avoid speculating.

V. Yes, you must be willing to relocate immediately. Also change your present occupation. Go south.

W. There doubtlessly will be. But the planetary signs now in strength may make you wish there had been none.

X. The stars are beaming joyfully upon you. It is your lot to succeed before fifty-seven more days are past.

Y. Avoid all speculations for now and your prospects will amend. There is at present, grounds for some alarm.

Z. Both will regret this fight. The lighter will be more skillful, but fate will vanquish the shortest of the two.

Table Twelve

A. Your doubtful years are the first four from this date, the second seven, and the fourth therefrom. Fate is silent about your thirty-fourth year.

B. You shall, if it is gold and silver you desire. You shall not, if marriage is your desire. You will sorely repent if you do.

C. Three hindrances are in your way. You will succeed in love, but certainly not in business dealings.

D. If you consult sincerely, your future mate's name begins with a T. You speak this name often, but do not yet know who.

E. A new doctor is required. Recovery will be delayed.

F. There is no fear of sudden termination, but many perils.

G. Born under the Moon sign, your fate is perplexing. You will experience much fickleness in life.

H. Yes, and they are presently blessed with good fortune.

I. If you seek news of a special day, it will be clear and warm. A season, mild and fruitful.

J. You will marry one whom you do not love deeply, yet prize highly. Wedlock brings a bountiful favor of fortune.

K. To wed someone now a stranger, fair and slender. You are destined to find great happiness in wedlock.

L. You may win, but this may prove to be the reverse. If possible, try to avoid this evil for it will bring turmoil.

M. You will win but little at play. Avoid it for the stars promise nothing but desperation and heartache.

N. You will take three trips before this year ends. One will commence within six weeks. Something important will happen.

O. Go north by land or west by sea. Dwell near theaters.

P. Your planet is passing its evil bearings and will soon be much more benevolent. Everything will be good in three days.

Q. Wednesday will always be fortunate. Tuesday will bring illness, and a closeness to death. Beware the ninth day after each new moon. Rejoice on each second day of the new moon.

R. Most friends will be female, but most flatter and are not to be trusted. Take care of what you speak in front of them.

S. They will never be recovered, but the thief will be punished in one year for another crime. Look in the earth if lost.

T. Illness in the immediate family, two changes of residence, one tedious journey; a death; a legacy; a wound; and a new friend.

U. You are destined to amass a substantial amount of wealth through dealing in chemicals and medicines.

V. Give your present position a fair evaluation before jumping to conclusions. Better omens are evident, and not far off.

W. Several changes will befall you. This year will be very gainful but full of worries. One month brings a happy surprise.

X. Three times an evil star prevails. Then you will gain.

Y. Your fortune is extremely favorable if you are sincere.

Z. Both will be injured, and one critically.

Table Thirteen

A. You will inherit wealth in later years, after sixty.

B. You will be well off while young, and gain great wealth by the time you are in middle age. Fifty-five is remarkable.

C. You will succeed if you can wait for twenty-two days.

D. O commences the name of one you are to wed. It is a long name and seldom ever spoken around you. For a thief, F.

E. Health is on the way. The critical period is over.

F. If you are able to pass fifty without peril, then long years of happiness await you. You will outlive all the family.

G. Your star is Mercury, and it foretells riches.

H. It will vary from faithful and then doubting.

I. The air will be cold in the spring, but foggy in the fall.

J. You will wander for three more years before settling down to one woman or man. Beware of the third summer after.

K. To marry a prominent person, someone in public life. You have either seen or know this person.

L. Your opponent is powerful and knowledgeable of the law, but justice will be on your side. You certainly will win.

M. This is not very fortunate, for Mercury indicates that you are to be badly taken advantage of through cheating.

N. Avoid travel at this time, for your fate is woeful.

O. You should not travel for at least two years. If you must, then head north and reside only in large cities.

P. The stars are insincere. You are not sufficiently earnest. Seek another answer in one week.

Q. One fifth day in a November within the next five years will resolve your fate for better or for worse.

R. Steadfast friends will be few, acquaintances many.

S. Part will be recovered. Look nearby for lost items.

T. Two promotions, three setbacks, one near imprisonment.

U. You will gain most by debate and controversy. Politics.

V. Yes, and as soon as humanly possible to avoid ill luck.

W. Your fate is rather uncertain. Little of the past has been good, but better days await you within six months.

X. The Moon says twice, once in four years, then again in two.

Y. You are destined to be wronged, for treachery is clearly visible in the future. Take heed and invest little.

Z. The bravest of the two will lose through deception.

Table Fourteen

A. Evil is most likely to take place before prosperity finally arrives. The bearing of the planets is remarkably good.

B. Every seventh year will be unkind to you, but you will enjoy your share of wealth and happiness thereafter.

C. The future promises everything. Bear with patience the fate that forces poverty upon you for a very short season.

D. If asking of a lover, try an A. Of a thief, try K or N.

E. A relapse, then improved health, finally a more critical period. A change in physicians is preferred by the patient.

F. The planets speak favorably of sixty-seven years or more.

G. Jupiter rules you. You will achieve much before you reach forty-nine, but will enjoy very little.

H. Your life bears many crosses, and there are enemies nearby. It is difficult to solve this question, for friends are few.

I. Rainy in the summer, frost in the fall.

J. Your fate in marriage will be one fraught with both the sweet and the bitter. You will generally be pleased.

K. Your mate will be respectable, light complexioned, and a quarreler. You will love this person, but also despise.

L. There are difficulties in the way, but you should come out well in the end. Do not trust others with all the details.

M. You are extremely unfortunate at games of chance. Beware of a dark man who will avoid you at all cost.

N. Begin no journey this month for the stars tell of danger.

O. You had better reside away from the water, and stay at home as much as possible. You are not destined to travel.

P. Mark well what takes place tomorrow. A great change is fast approaching. Your day will be most fortunate.

Q. The fifteenth of every month will be of the greatest consequence in life and actions. Fridays are most fortunate.

R. Hypocrisy and deceit are your lot when consulting those you feel are your closest friends. You possess but one.

S. A female was the thief. Do not plan on recovering it.

T. Marriage (if you are of the proper age), and a totally unexpected change in your pursuits. Expect family deaths.

U. Seek your fortune in the law, religion, or even politics.

V. Your fate in this particular matter is inconsistent. You must use your own good judgment, and go by past experience.

W. Your best friend will bring this. Your future is as changeable as the Moon. Prepare for many drastic revisions.

X. Good and evil are evenly divided. By practicing caution, most of the evil influence can be eliminated and avoided.

Y. You will be close to giving up hope at least three times. Don't though, because fortune will favor you in the end.

Z. A surprise awaits you. The expected victor will lose.

Table Fifteen

A. Both male and female consultants will be fortunate within one month from this day. One year brings even more.

B. Wealthy in love, yes, but financially, no.

C. Your mind changes as you seek this answer. The planets shine upon you, and fate will be good in all ways.

D. Your future partner's name begins with an S, and it is not an uncommon name. If you ask of a thief, try M.

E. There is considerable danger because of improper treatment.

F. Guard your health carefully against diseases. You should easily reach a reasonable age and experience much happiness.

G. Mars is your planet. You are destined for wealth, but little happiness, and honor, but with few true friendships.

H. Trust but very few of your so-called friends.

I. The weather will be pleasant on that particular day.

J. To wed someone of dark complexion, born in a foreign land. You will be happy, and marry into money.

K. Your fate is seen by the planets as most perplexing. Your marriage adventure will be so accordingly.

L. You will face and defeat a false witness, and suffer through a multitude of petty troubles. Some planets show irritability.

M. There will be much disappointment and sorrow even though you are certain to win. Watch carefully for troubles.

N. Evil signs will show themselves three times. After this, there is hope for safe travel. Wait patiently.

O. Go only to the east if you expect to gain. Choose only seaport towns and cities if at all possible.

P. The signs vary extensively, but your wishes are far from the most promising. Reconsider your needs.

Q. Thursday will be your unfortunate day, while Wednesday will bring forth great tidings. You will have cause to pray.

R. Cherish your few friends for many enemies are evident.

S. Stolen things are not destined to be returned to you. Search for lost items in small jars or other receptacles.

T. The next seven years will be the most fortunate part of your entire life. Your ill-fated past is now completed.

U. Selling is the most likely trade for you. Deal in something liquid: Liquor, syrup, wines, etc., will bring success.

V. Go quickly for there are signs of gain if you do.

W. You will face four serious problems because of a bitter enemy. Then success will certainly come.

X. A great change will take place in two years.

Y. Take advantage of good fortune while you are able. There are signs of rejoicing, but do not be imprudent.

Z. A peacemaker will try to part them five times, but with little success. The taller of the two will eventually win.

Table Sixteen

A. A great part of your life will be embittered by inconsistency, but you will experience the ultimate after forty.

B. Your destiny is as changeable as the elements. You are fated to suffer much depression and a multitude of joy, but no money.

C. The signs of fortune are few but they speak well for you.

D. The one you will marry begins with an E, a lover with T.

E. Some unorthodox treatment may well effect a cure. The patient is presently in danger. Have faith.

F. Expect maladies in your twenty-second, thirty-third, and forty-fifty years. A fair chance for long life is predicted.

G. Venus is your favorite planet. You are destined to travel, and then go into business. You will be rich in substance.

H. They are in trouble and grieving, but faithful to you.

I. If tomorrow, cloudy and rain. If another day, foul.

J. A painful, sorrowful union. If you marry twice, your destiny will bring slightly better things.

K. You will marry three times. One mate will be wealthy, one beloved, and one hateful and a plague to happiness.

L. The signs are those of safety, but not of profit. You will not enrich yourself by these proceedings, but you will win.

M. Beware of gambling for the stars speak of failures.

N. Twenty-eight days will bring forth evil, but things will change for the better before the year is out, and you will travel.

O. Try not to tempt the dangers of traveling. Stay near the place of your birth all of your life.

P. Enemies are manifest, but a close and true friend approaches. This person, whom you know quite well, will save the day.

Q. Sunday is your most fortunate day, and you will die on that day. Your birthdate is unfortunate. Do no planning then.

R. Many slanderers and backbiters are close at hand. But the planets tell of one dear friend who is faithful through all.

S. If theft has been committed, look for a young person, one with a quick tongue, sharp-minded, and fast-paced.

T. Love, three marriages; traveling; damage by flood; loss of a close friend; and finally wonderful news of good fortune.

U. You are indeed fortunate, and should follow the footsteps of some noted person.

V. Not at the present time, but surely in three months.

W. A great change is coming within the next twenty-nine days.

X. You will be terribly mortified and hurt by someone you dearly love. Then fortune smiles and you will marry wealth.

Y. Yes, but only after several disappointments and anxieties.

Z. That a battle will really take place is dubious, but if one does, the weaker will ultimately win.

Table Seventeen

A. Your planet wanes after you reach the age of forty. Make the best of her favorable gifts and you will not die in obscurity.

B. You will have many problems until you reach middle age. Then fate will be kind as riches and dignities are your lot.

C. Do not be depressed for the goodly planets proclaim a run of lucky fortune. Seize the better moments while you can.

D. The initial of a lover, F. Of a thief, D.

E. A speedy relapse, but all sickness signs will disappear within one long and tedious month.

F. Perverse omens will thwart you at every turn, and the planets are opposed, but do not despair. You will have as you wish.

G. Your planet is Saturn, and it brings heaps of money.

H. Why doubt your friends' truthfulness? They are discreet and capable of being faithful to you under all conditions.

I. Deep snow during that fateful wintry day you think of.

J. You will marry someone who is virtuous, but this match will be violently opposed by a friend. You already know who it is.

K. Harassed and perplexed by fickle fortune. This sign indicates very little true love coming.

L. A dark person will prevent you from winning the law suit.

M. You should take heed of this warning for there are more signs of losing than of winning at the present time.

N. The stars warn of danger by drowning if your present plans are not radically revised. Mishaps are also predicted by land.

O. Where you intend to travel is of little importance for the planets indicate good fortune.

P. The omens are bright and cheerful concerning the day you think about. Eliminate all deep anxiety about this.

Q. One of the most notable days in your life will be the twenty-third of July, but Tuesdays will always be prosperous.

R. Two friends are seen by the stars, one elderly. But the signs show generally more enmity than friendship.

S. You will find the stolen goods, but will be unable to recover them. All hopes of restitution are futile.

T. Two serious accidents; a fire; a change of friends; a fateful trip to a foreign land; and two years of extremely good luck.

U. In laboring trades where you supervise others.

V. If you wish to relocate then do so immediately and without hesitation. Any delay will foment strife and troubles.

W. Three stars favor you. There will be much success.

X. Yes but it will vex you because of its suddenness.

Y. Yes. The planet Venus gives much pleasure after a delay.

Z. They must not be allowed to fight, for death will claim at least one of them, and possibly both.

Table Eighteen

A. Your most perverse years will be between the ages of eighteen and twenty-four. Imprisonment may be near. Beware also of your thirty-seventh year, for it is dangerous.

B. You will become wealthy soon through fortune's gifts, but it will just as quickly be lost for all time.

C. The signs indicated in the stars are doubtful.

D. E is the letter of a name concerning love and friendship.

E. Faint, indeed, are the hopes of a full recovery.

F. The signs are ambiguous. Success is promised but a short life is possible. Be alert to dangers.

G. Mars is the planet of your fate. You will have a remarkable life, with much difficulty but great gain.

H. The signs foretell cheating and fraud.

I. Cold, snow, and sleet if in the winter. But warm, calm and fruitful if in the spring or summer.

J. Do not be too impetuous for this may prove your ruin.

K. Let them beware of ingratitude and unfaithfulness.

L. The omens are favorable toward your winning this.

M. Assuredly stand in dread of a great loss of finances.

N. Do nothing in haste. Think it over carefully.

O. Westward and northward, avoiding the other parts of the globe. Dwell near navigable rivers. Do not locate permanently.

P. The stars look upon you in deceit. Beware of that day.

Q. The two best weeks for you are those falling between the new and the full Moon. Wednesday will be notable, but not good.

R. The stars speak only of many friends.

S. Many more troubles are due to soon come. Your most prized possessions will never be suitably recovered.

T. You will enjoy only the sunshine of success.

U. Some skilled trade where you cater to the whims of the rich. Also traveling and bartering with foreigners.

V. Evil news will soon be upon you. There is little cause for alarm. Do not change in haste.

W. An obstacle will suddenly arise unexpectedly. Once this is overcome and swept aside, expect great successes.

X. Envious persons surround you but it may improve.

Y. The answer to this is not attainable for you are quite insincere in asking. You do not believe in the power herein.

Z. The short and corpulent individual will surely win.

Table Nineteen

A. Perpetual troubles are your fate in early life, but age will open a prosperous era and bring wealth to you.

B. You are indeed fortunate in moneymaking, but do not devote all time to this. Seek peace of mind, instead.

C. Delays will generally prove to be the obstacles in your road to success. Do not pursue your desires so slowly.

D. For the name of a lover, try G. In all other cases, V.

E. There is absolutely no doubt about it. Recovery.

F. A moderate age is foretold. Live well while you can.

G. Venus rules. You will not be extremely rich, but neither will you ever want for material things. Moderate success are seen.

H. There is a loss of friendship seen, but after troubles are finally overcome, good luck and many close friends.

I. Watch and prepare for foul weather. The planets are evil.

J. Prudence must be utilized in making the proper selection. There will be much personal attraction, but little love.

K. She is determined to make a bad choice, because of strong pressures by friends. The threatened fate is well deserved.

L. The trial will prove to be ambiguous, and a foe will try to ruin you through this legal effort. It will not succeed.

M. Nothing can save you from the disappointing losses.

N. Take no trips for at least three weeks. There is danger.

O. Your entire future fate depends on the journey you will make in the next seven months. Eastern travel brings honor and fame.

P. Protected by the planetary signs, it will be prosperous.

Q. Friday is a day of woe. Thursday a day of excitement. Expect the fifteenth day of any month to be remarkable in some way.

R. The planets signify the friendship of some prominent personality. But a secret enemy is also denoted.

S. Stolen items are most likely to be recovered.

T. Marriage, an increase in family, a tedious lawsuit, one unfortunate year, and three wonderfully lucky years.

U. Law will be your best field. You are well fitted for it.

V. Change either your place of business or your home.

W. Many unexpected changes. The stars presage safety.

X. The omens will shortly change for the better.

Y. Perilous but not unfortunate. Act accordingly.

Z. The combat will never actually take place.

Table Twenty

A. One-third of your career will be unavoidably sad, and full of frustration. The balance will be extremely fruitful.

B. Many snares must first be successfully encountered.

C. Moderately so, if you ask in sincerity of the stars.

D. Your future partner's name begins with an A.

E. Something extremely favorable is presently implied.

F. After a multitude of illnesses, good health and a long life will surely be yours.

G. Mercury is your planet and it signifies that many paths of wealth and happiness are opening before your very eyes.

H. There is little doubt of it. Do not be suspicious.

I. Flooding in the winter, storms in the autumn, hail in the spring, and cloudy in the summer.

J. You will be happy in wedlock provided that you treat your mate fairly, and practice fidelity.

K. The bonds of marriage will force this person to respect and admire the one who causes the greatest happiness in life.

L. There are some signs of confusion so be watchful during all legal proceedings. Someone owes you a favor.

M. It may well produce much needed money at this time.

N. There are signs of misfortune evident. The planets are clouded and unlucky. Take great care if you do travel.

O. You would do best by remaining in one location, but if you absolutely must travel, head due north.

P. The stars promise success and who shall question them?

Q. Wednesday will no doubt be the most remarkable.

R. Few real friends, but many acquaintances. Enemies galore.

S. Stolen things are not to be found. Do not hope for it.

T. You are fated to meet with prosperity, contentment, and peace of mind after a long struggle with adverse forces.

U. In any reputable business enterprise.

V. Relocation between the new and full Moon will bring good.

W. There are few causes for alarm. Expect good fortune.

X. The planets signify a great deal of trouble.

Y. There is some danger from enemies. The planets indicate problems, but changes for the better will commence in one month.

Z. The stoutest will win all.

Table Twenty-One

A. The favors of fortune will manifest themselves while you are youthful. Later life may bring misfortune.

B. Your fate, while it does not presage an enormous amount of wealth, is extremely fortunate. Be contented with this.

C. Do not allow your desires to be inordinate. You will succeed quite well where money is concerned.

D. If asking about a thief, try the letter G. But if about love or marriage, try an M.

E. The illness will change to something unexpected. After a long struggle, recovery is quite certain.

F. If you live past forty, life will be safe.

G. The Moon influences you strongly. You will do much traveling, experience frequent distress, and be overcome with grief.

H. There is some hindrance in this matter. But honesty will most often reign supreme. Never fear a true friend.

I. Heat and terrible humidity will prevail.

J. You should ask for no more than a happy union.

K. Contentment and ultimate happiness is the lot to expect.

L. A friend will foresake you, and better omens will appear only after cares are overcome. The suit will be troublesome.

M. The signs indicate winning. Good fortune is before you.

N. Your fate is unsettled, and prone to changes. Be careful.

O. If you roam, return to where you presently are.

P. It surely will. The stars in the heavens proclaim good.

Q. The eighteenth day of each month will be notable, both for good and evil. Monday is your most fortunate day of the week.

R. One enemy is evident, a dark-haired person. This is evenly balanced by a trustworthy friend with light hair.

S. More than one thief is involved in this. Part of the stolen goods will be retrieved eventually.

T. You will at first be worse off than at present, but, the omens of good fortune prevail. After a grievous malady, success and good fortune will be yours forever.

U. Fortune will favor almost anything you attempt.

V. Go quickly. Do not hesitate. The stars forewarn you of a dastardly event to take place soon if you stay.

W. There will first be some evil then, in three months, a cessation and a beneficial change.

X. Evil signs are visible but this trouble will quickly be no more. A stroke of fortune will strike unexpectedly.

Y. One investment may prove successful beyond your wildest expectations. But this will take another year at least.

Z. A strange factor enters into the picture. After this is taken care of, the victor will be the tall, rosy-cheeked man.

Table Twenty-Two

A. Your rise in life will be due to mysterious circumstances. This will not take place until you have passed the age of forty-one.

B. Something may imperceptibly arise to alter your fortune, but as it now stands, the stars do not look very good.

C. Some difficulties are near, but they are not insurmountable if you are able to persevere. Some signs are fortunate.

D. There are three competitors for your love. The initials are R, T, and W. You know only two of them.

E. Recovery is most certain after a short wait.

F. You will have many close calls with death in infancy, but you will survive to live on. Old age will bring happiness.

G. Mercury rules your destiny and portends happiness while young, and security when older.

H. Flattery and untruth are seen. Do not believe this one.

I. Bad. Plan on a change of dates. Try a Wednesday.

J. You are a lover of many and cannot settle down to one. You will not have many opportunities to marry very well.

K. To wed a rich, elderly person, instead of the young one presently being considered.

L. The lawsuit will be postponed and then forgotten.

M. Expect serious losses at first. Then possible wins.

N. Take no trips if you seek health, wealth, and happiness.

O. If you must travel, go to well-populated areas.

P. It may, if you remain discreet. Otherwise it will be one of the most unpleasant days of your entire life.

Q. Your chief days of fortune will be Tuesday and Saturday. Your most prosperous time will be while the Moon is in Taurus.

R. Three certain friends, and one backbiting enemy.

S. You are doomed to be a victim and will not recover anything.

T. An illegitimate offspring; severe illness; three long and fruitful trips; a change in business; and great overall gains.

U. You will be enriched by an inheritance and will not have to worry about going into any business ventures.

V. Do not relocate under any circumstances. Give your present place more of a fair trial. It will prove prosperous.

W. The stars speak of drastic changes in one month for good. Then another in two months will prove disappointing.

X. An ominous planet overwhelms your youthful destiny, and sadly influences your middle age. You will ultimately drink from the cup of joy, but only after much woe.

Y. Some woman will prove a burden to your successful speculations. You will be cast down, but will rise again in one year.

Z. Bribes and lies will influence the outcome. One will eventually flee from the other. Depend on the stronger.

Table Twenty-Three

A. Between fifteen and twenty-five it will be stormy. But during your thirties, expect the best. Later life will be good.

B. Evidently not at all, for the signs are ominous enough.

C. You shall quickly attain that which you now seek.

D. If you desire to know of a thief, it is C. A lover, E.

E. Your friend is sick, but will not die for many more years.

F. Your present disposition threatens to embitter you, and as a result, shorten your life. Curb this feeling of hatred.

G. Mars is your faithful guide throughout life. It signifies a strange, remarkable fate. Be cautious.

H. Your friend is truer than most could hope for.

I. Fine and clear weather whenever this event takes place.

J. Marry later in life or you may have cause for regret.

K. To marry well and end up a widow or a widower with many wonderful memories, cash on hand, and youth.

L. It would be best to seek some means of settlement out of the court room in this serious matter.

M. The planets smile favorably, yet you will seldom find much luck in a game of chance because of swindlers.

N. Do not pursue this matter for the stars portend danger.

O. Avoid travel whenever possible, but if you must, then go where there are sparsely populated towns.

P. Planetary signs are against you now. It will be a bad day.

Q. Monday and Saturday will be most fortunate, the latter being the most eventful of the two.

R. Many more friends than enemies. Take heart in this.

S. If you look for stolen gold or silver it will never be recovered because it has been melted down and sold.

T. The stars proclaim many faithful friends will join with you in some major investment. It will succeed overwhelmingly.

U. Work in handicrafts, most probably metals.

V. You cannot relocate soon enough. Move immediately as the planets are preparing surprising good fortune for you.

W. Can you not recognize the danger signs before you? Be most careful and much heartache can be avoided. Then comes success.

X. You are warned by the heavenly bodies to be more than careful with those you love. Look to their welfare.

Y. There is evidence of trouble arising unexpectedly. You should be vigilant and then you will prosper more in the long run.

Z. The strife will be extremely cruel. The one you think will be the victor will lose his life.

Table Twenty-Four

A. Your best fortune is in the immediate future.

B. It will be a long time in coming for evil omens now predominate around you. Be prepared and alert for changes.

C. Not of love or money, but otherwise, the odds are with you.

D. Watch for the letter K if it be love you are concerned with; if any other thing, the letter O will be correct.

E. More than one relapse is foreshadowed for the patient is being improperly treated.

F. The planets foretell of a very long and productive life.

G. Mars is your ruling planet. Many sudden strokes of good fortune are visible. An eminent title will eventually be yours.

H. The stars are favorably placed. Expect truth from your friends, for they are all sincere.

I. If you ask of a particular day it will be pleasant.

J. A prosperous marriage to a favorite of both sexes.

K. To wed a clever, deceptive person who is jealous.

L. You may be able to overcome organized conspiracies and win.

M. This always brings you trouble. Avoid it when possible.

N. The stars foreshadow melancholy because of an impending misfortune. Ask this question later in the month.

O. If you must travel, let it be inland, near mountains. Avoid freshwater lakes and rivers.

P. If you pay strict attention to certain particulars, it will.

Q. The tenth of each month will be remarkable for you, and Tuesdays prove to be your luckiest day of the week.

R. Enemies is the candid reply for the stars indicate deceit.

S. They will be returned after a short, emotional period.

T. There are many scenes of violence and danger. Then a friendly star appears to aid you in all endeavors.

U. Deal only in the produce of the earth, especially fruits.

V. You are under the control of a tremendous power. Relocate only with extreme caution, and during the rise of the Moon.

W. Expect drastic changes, one of particular importance.

X. Your planetary signs are changing to a more fortunate bearing. Something wonderful is destined in the near future.

Y. Benevolent constellations assure fulfillment if you can be patient for one more month.

Z. The one with red hair and green eyes will win.

Table Twenty-Five

A. You are destined to suffer between the ages of twenty-one and thirty-one. Persecution will prevail for seven years. Then you will enjoy life from this point on. Old age will be happy.

B. It is not ordained for you to become wealthy.

C. You will be thwarted five times before attaining every sincere desire. Do not give up hope for the signs are good.

D. If of anyone other than a lover, try L. If of a marriage partner, or a lover, try S.

E. A relapse is coming due to a lack of cautiousness. There have been serious blunders in treatment.

F. If you are able to get past the age of thirty-five, then will fate shine upon you, and you will live long.

G. Near imprisonment, but saved by a stroke of luck. You will have evil fortune for ten years, and then things change.

H. Your friend is presently traveling. Upon his return you will find out this answer.

I. Much better than you would hope for.

J. You will marry a highly accomplished person, but only after having tasted the fruits of bitter despair in love.

K. To wed a tall stranger and to inherit a great deal of wealth. But you are destined to suffer through much infidelity.

L. You may lose through the deceit of a friend, but the tide can be turned in your favor by being more alert during proceedings.

M. You are now under evil planetary influences. It behooves you to be more cautious than usual in this important matter.

N. There is one approaching. Take advantage of it.

O. Anywhere you desire, for nothing but good can come of it.

P. It certainly will be, for three planets speak in favor.

Q. Of all seven weekdays, Tuesday is your most remarkable. This day will bring forth events to determine your entire future.

R. Definitely more enemies although those few friends are faithful to the bitter end. You can rely on them for assistance.

S. Give up your quest after things stolen. They are not destined for recovery.

T. Long trips, a promotion, one year of misfortune followed by five more of unusual goodness. You may be endangered by fire.

U. You will surely succeed in dealing with ornamental goods. Consider paintings or other artistic work.

V. Beware of any hazardous enterprise and take great precautions before making any type of move.

W. There will be three major changes, all for the good.

X. It will no doubt get worse because of your attitudes.

Y. In all probability they will for you have invested wisely in accordance with the wishes of the stars. You cannot fail.

Z. The darker of the three will defeat the other two.

Table Twenty-Six

A. There are two portents of sorrow, and one exceedingly happy omen. You will assuredly be happy in the final analysis.

B. You will attain a great deal of wealth at a relatively youthful age. The stars are wholly on your side.

C. Beware of your present actions or you will attain nothing but compounded troubles. Look well to your desires.

D. Look for one whose name begins with T for all things.

E. Recovery is doubtful at this time but do not give up hope.

F. Pursue a path of sobriety and temperance. Avoid abuse of health and a long useful life will be yours.

G. Venus protects you against all forms of evil. You will achieve adequate success if you are cautious around others.

H. The planets tell of flattery and untruths. Beware of the one you are friendliest with at the present time.

I. If you ask of a special day, it is destined to be wet.

J. First a great adventure in love, then an unhappy marriage.

K. Great frustration after two years of bliss.

L. You are destined to win a large settlement of property.

M. Gambling comes naturally to you. You will win heavily.

N. No trips will be fortunate. Wait one week before going.

O. If you must travel at all, go to the closest city.

P. No, it will not, because you are planning evil things.

Q. Deep trouble is proclaimed for Wednesdays, and luck will make an appearance on Saturdays. The seventh of any month is good.

R. You have but one tested friend. Beware of deceivers.

S. If things have been stolen, the thieves are far off.

T. A smiling star looks fondly upon your next seven years. But after that time, prepare for troubles and misfortune.

U. A partnership with a reliable friend will prove a benefit in the lending field, or in investments.

V. Yes, if you are to avoid bribery, and falsehood.

W. Something of considerable importance is going to happen to you. Expect this event to take place in less than three months.

X. Evil shows in the heavens. The planets presently deny a change for the better.

Y. Not at all unless you stop taking other people's advice in such matters. Look to your own intuition.

Z. Three times you will face immediate danger, but then you shall vanquish the other individual with a mighty blow.